Letters
to
Jennifer:
A collection of (painfully) true tales

D0733392

Shawn Carrier

ISBN: 9798436615127
Cover design: Lauren Moore at ©Word Garden Studio

Acknowledgements

Many readers skip the acknowledgements page, which in my opinion is a waste of good money. When you buy a book you are *paying* for every page, so you should *read* every page. If you skip the acknowledgements, you are actually spending more money per page. You do the math. So for those of you who faithfully begin with this page, I will attempt to make it interesting and give you more value for your investment.

Thank you, dear Reader, for making it this far.

Thank you, Lauren, for the cover design. It's simple. It's beautiful. It's simply beautiful – just like you.

Thank you, Lauren and Brittany, for your technical expertise, your creative ideas, and your fake laughs on the not-so-funny stories. You made it much easier to decide which tales needed additional embellishing (as compared to the *original* embellishing). By the way, my fake laugh is much more advanced than yours. I would show you how to polish it up, but then it would be more difficult to spot where the editing is needed.

Thank you, James, for being the best IT guy in the world – no, in the entire universe – and my biggest supporter. Without you, I would still be writing in long hand on a legal pad with a #2 pencil. You laughed at every single one of my stories. It was so sweet of you to pretend. You are my hero. I hope that someday I can be as good a person as you think I am.

Most of all, thank You, Heavenly Father, my Lord and my God, for blessing me more than anything I could have ever asked or imagined.

.

Introduction

This book is written in memory of my friend and coworker Jennifer Gregory: the bravest person I ever knew. She fought a 10-year battle with metastatic breast cancer and bore her struggles with incomparable grace and dignity. Several years ago, Jennifer was on leave for a few weeks getting treatments and I sent her weekly updates of office facts, never gossip, always facts. Always. Facts. Eventually, the office facts just dried up. There is only so much one can relate each week about office life: Hi, Jennifer – today it was raining but I couldn't see it because I don't have a window. *Boring*. I ate lunch in the cafeteria. They served meatloaf and mashed potatoes. It was good. *Yawn*. I had to load 6 packages of paper in the printer. *z-z-z*. A few messages like this and Jennifer would've stopped checking her mail.

Desperate times call for desperate measures. I began to draw on my rich, vast storehouse of silly anecdotes provided by old friends, lovable neighbors, and my crazy, adorable family. Oh, and my #1 goofball – me. It must have worked. When Jennifer returned to work, the cards and letters kept going out - at her request. "Just because I am back in the office doesn't mean you have to stop sending me those stories," she said to me. I couldn't make her better, but I could try to lighten her load. I felt it was my duty to keep Jennifer entertained and her heart light, so I kept sending her weekly, mostly true, stories of some of the weird, dumb and silly things that have happened to my family members, friends, and me since the beginning of time – the 1950s. It was an honor to do this small thing for her.

Our letter sending and receiving arrangement worked great for a few short, sweet years. Then in 2022, my courageous friend left her body of pain and received ultimate healing in Heaven.

Thank you, Jennifer, for being my example, my encourager, and most of all – my friend.

I still have a deep longing to continue writing letters to her. This desire has given birth to *Letters to Jennifer*, which is a compilation of a handful of the stories I sent to her and some that didn't make the mail in time. I think she would approve.

As you read there are some important things to consider:
First of all, my English teachers had a rule about numbers in an essay. If the numbers were single digits they should be spelled out (numerals), or something like that. But my letters to Jennifer were quick and informal and I don't think she ever judged me for typing numbers instead of numerals in her mail.

Second, my English teachers had a rule about contractions in an essay. It would not be good writing. We should not do it. So, do not. But my letters to Jennifer were quick and informal and I don't think she ever would've judged me for using contractions in her mail when I shouldn't've.

Third, I know how to use good grammar and punctuation; I know what gerunds, split infinitives and incomplete sentences are. I know that a sentence shouldn't end with a preposition. And I don't care. I have simply chosen not to be correct in some cases. Sometimes grammatical errors are more appropriate for the settings in the following pages and incomplete sentences are a Lot. More. Fun. Also, in my defense, auto correct and spell check have dulled my senses to spelling errors over the years.

Finally, these stories are not fiction. They are true. Mostly. 'Mostly' in this case means that all the stories are true, but some are truer than others. Sometimes I might exaggerate and write 'a million' when one hundred thousand is more accurate, but for the most part, they really happened. Jennifer often asked me for more details about them (especially if the subject was Sasquatch) and if I had created them out of my imagination, I wouldn't have known how to respond to her, or even remembered what she was referring to. I had to maintain some level of integrity, so I had to keep these tall tales honest. Mostly.

Unfortunately, many of these tales are so ridiculous or bizarre, they don't require much embellishment. I will let the reader decide which stories those are. Some of these true tales are extremely embarrassing and all of them are about people I know, people who know me, and … me. For this reason, all names (except Jennifer's) have been changed to protect the innocent, the ignorant, and my face.

A merry heart doeth good like a medicine.
Proverbs 17:22 (KJV)

Dedication

For James

You never give up on me

and you never let me settle

for less than I can be.

Table of Contents

JASPER

Dear Jennifer,

Did I ever tell you about my cat? My friend's cat had a litter and I got the beauty of the bunch. He was jet black from head to tail and was just the cutest little thing. And he was free. But I found out very quickly that getting a free cat is equivalent to replacing all your natural teeth with dental implants. The cost ends up being about the same.

Jasper began life as Jasmine. We were assured that this kitty was a female (and I'm embarrassed to confess that I couldn't tell the difference). Imagine my surprise when we took Jasmine to have her spayed and the vet called with a little announcement. "The bad news is that Jasmine is really Jasper. The good news is that neutering is cheaper than spaying."

In retrospect, after his parts were removed, there was really no reason to rename him. By that point, he was as much a Jasmine as he was a Jasper. But I was in shock at the time and let them change her/his name in the files without thinking it through.

Jasper was very entertaining and acted like a regular cat – most of the time. Sometimes he would jump in my lap for some lovin' and just about the time I was beginning to trust him and love on him a little, he would sink his fangs into my arm and run off. Maybe he just preferred negative attention. Maybe he had a strong desire to speed through a couple of his lives.

I think he was bipolar.

For those times Jasper was just pure evil I kept a little rolled up newspaper with a rubber band on each end. He got a little pop on the tail when he was a bad boy. I had trouble keeping up with my little newspaper roll, so I was forced to make new ones all the time. And why? Jasper insisted on being evil sometimes and refused to learn the lesson. One day we were rearranging the living room furniture and discovered a pile of twenty-seven rolled up newspapers behind the couch. Jasper wasn't just an evil cat – he was an evil genius. He got a little treat for being so intelligent.

He and I had a love/hate relationship – he loved it when he got on my nerves and I hated it when I couldn't get one over on him. His favorite thing to annoy me was to jump up on my stomach when I was taking a Sunday afternoon snooze on the couch. First of all, it just about scared me to death to be awakened that way. A twelve pound pounce can be rather painful. But part two of his ploy was to get all comfortable and adjusted on me so that his rear end was pointing toward my face. Part three was to tickle my nose with a flick of his tail. He enjoyed that very much. It didn't take an animal expert to see how part four would play out. So, nap time would be over after that because I was no longer willing to remain flat on my back in victim position. I might not know about cat parts, but I can anticipate being asphyxiated by a green cloud when the setup is right. And a long tail tickling my nose wasn't conducive to a good nap anyway.

Jasper lived with us through all 9 of his lives. Gracious sakes, some of them were long ones. I will share some 'Jasper Tales' with you over the next few weeks.

JASPER GOES TO THE VET

Dear Jennifer,

It was time for Jasper's shots and as much as he hated going to the vet, I hated it even more. I was the one who had to take him there.

Step 1: Put him in the cat carrier. That activity required about 2 hours, but I knew this going in so I started in plenty of time. Jasper was the smartest cat in the world. He knew every trick for NOT getting into that carrier and could perform countless acrobatic stunts to keep me from inserting him in there. He was a lean and long cat, so he could fit easily enough through the opening. But he simply wasn't having it. A seasoned cat owner friend of mine had told me the 'simple' way was to put the carrier on its end and then basically 'pour' Jasper into it. Jasper wasn't pourable. He had already heard about that trick before I even started.

His first maneuver was to become the letter X. Capital X, not lower case x. In the capital X position, he could make himself extremely wide and large enough to keep me from pouring him through the doorway. This was quickly followed by his second ploy, which was to grab the four corners of the doorway while in the X position, so if I tried to push him through, his body behaved much like a trampoline. He was quite stretchable. Jasper also had command of the English language and could say a few words quite clearly. Some non-cat people might only hear meowing, but I could plainly understand when he vocalized the word "Nooooooooooo". For non-cat people, Jasper's negative response might sound much like a wounded coyote howling at the moon: loud and long and painful. And Jasper was pretty vocal about not getting into the cat carrier. What I needed was a distraction. "Jasper, sweet kitty, would you like a treat?" At the sound of the T word Jasper momentarily forgot himself, giving me just enough time to perform my now famous Cat Half Nelson. I shoved him inside and locked the door. Sorry, Jasper, this hurts me more than it does you. But I wasn't dishonest; I squeezed a treat through the bars of his prison. And it really *did* hurt me more than it hurt him because he bit me several times. I certainly didn't bite him, so he was in no pain.

And that was just preparing to get ready to go to the vet's office. We hadn't even made it to the car yet. I had to hear about his problems for the entire trip to the vet's office, which wasn't nearly close enough to our house. Jasper had such lung capacity he sustained the word 'Noooooooooo' for the duration of the 20-minute drive. And his 'Noooooooooo' was spoken with overtones which I understood all too well. I would be paying for this for a long time.

Step 2: See the vet. Jasper became a cartoon cat once inside the examining room. He could actually cling to the popcorn ceiling with all four claws. But not for long. He was desperate and I actually felt sorry for him. With only an examining table and an uncomfortable plastic chair for humans, the small room didn't provide many hiding places. I whispered his name and he saw me slide my purse across my lap and toward my knees. This provided a small cat canyon, just wide enough for Jasper to hide in. He jumped in my lap and cowered behind my purse. The canyon was wide enough, but not nearly long enough. Most of him was hanging off my lap. Note that I described him as lean and *long*. I cooed softly to him and told him this was for his own health and well-being. We were at the vet's office to extend his 9 lives. He would thank me someday. I didn't believe this any more than he did.

Dr. Shepherd came through the door and I felt Jasper go rigid. I was thinking I would have to use him as a doorstop from then on. Then I betrayed him. I revealed his hiding place and put him up on the table. Jasper gave me the evil eye that said "A gift or several will be waiting for you sometime in the next few days".

Finally, the visit was over and Dr. Shepherd thanked me and turned to leave the examining room. Oh, no – I was not allowing him to leave me alone to box up my cat. I insisted

4

that someone help me get this Tasmanian devil back into the carrier. Dr. Shepherd looked at me like I was the most spoiled and petted baby he had ever seen. So with just a little smirk he took Jasper in his arms to show me how easy it was to pour a cat into a cage. And he was exactly right. After he called in a technician, the secretary and the drink machine guy for an assist.

JASPER GETS A BATH

Dear Jennifer,

It was a pretty summer day. The birds were singing, the bees were buzzing, and Hubby was excited. And not in a good way. He had found a flea on Jasper. This was a real puzzler because Jasper was an indoor kitty. I'm not sure if he had ever touched a blade of grass in his entire lives, however many he had used up by this point.

But there is never one flea, so I had to give Jasper a bath. This happened years ago and I still don't know why it was up to me to wash this cat. I wasn't the one who found the flea. What happened to the finders-keepers rule? Maybe I lost the coin toss.

I knew this would be akin to putting Jasper in a cat carrier, only wetter, so I tried to prepare myself. I put on my oldest, nastiest shorts and tee shirt. I pulled my hair back and lined the bathroom with old towels. Maybe they weren't old towels yet, but they would probably qualify as old towels by the end of this activity. I filled the tub with a couple inches of nice warm soapy water. It looked comfy cozy to me. But I guess I wasn't looking at it with cat eyes. I did everything I could to prepare a nice bath and then considered reading *War and Peace* to delay the inevitable. But a flea was waiting and it wasn't going away on its own. Jasper had a beautiful coat, and if I were a flea, that's the cat I would pick to live on.

Hubby asked if there was anything he could do. Okay, for starters, you can wash this cat. Well, no, he meant could he run and fetch for me, pray for me, etc. Thanks, pal.

I found Jasper sunning himself in a window, loving life, and looking down on those poor cats outside who didn't have their own designer litter box. He didn't have a care in the world – he certainly didn't care that he was host to at least one parasite. I picked him up and talked baby talk to him. He purred. Poor dear. He should have been just a little suspicious. Hubby closed (and probably hermetically sealed) the bathroom door as soon as Jasper and I were inside. I still talked goo-goo sweet baby to Jasper as I stepped into the tub and sat down on the side, just as I would for my human babies. No, that's not quite true. I didn't go anywhere near this much prep time with them to get them clean. The plan was to ease this flea-bitten varmint (I've always heard that expression, but never had an occasion to use it until now) into the concept of getting wet and soapy. Then I gently lowered my kitty into the nice warm soapy water. "Nooooooooooo". His English was always so good.

Immediately, this was a baptism gone horribly wrong. A drenched cat came up out of the water and in half a nanosecond had completely wrapped himself around my thigh. Well, I sure didn't see that one coming. I looked like I was wearing a thick black garter. How can I describe peeling a wet cat off my leg? How can I describe peeling a cat off my leg when he is determined to NOT let go? I had to give him points for endurance. He simply was not getting back in that water.

But I was bigger than he was and by now, just as hairy. We ended up fighting a little bit, and I sort of won because I had to demonstrate my power and authority over this animal. The first chapter of Genesis makes it clear that I have dominion over animals and that included Jasper. Unfortunately, Jasper had not read Genesis.

I didn't see what the big deal was. Surely, that pretty smelling bath water couldn't be any worse than cat spit. He never seemed to mind covering himself with that.

I washed and washed and talked baby talk and sang silly songs. He might have been singing along with me. It was hard to understand his words during this phase of the program. I washed my kitty until I was sure there were no fleas still breathing, and then I picked him up and wrapped him in a soft warm towel. I dried his fur and talked more baby talk and told him what a good kitty he was. Liar. He spent the rest of the day with his back to me, grooming and licking himself to get all that pleasant soap smell off his fur. I guess he really did prefer cat spit to soap.

Now it was my turn to get cleaned up. I didn't fight to stay out of a hot soapy shower. After a day and a half in there I finally felt clean enough to get out and dry off with a clean fresh towel or seven. I think most of the cat hairs were rinsed off by then.

After Jasper was dry, sufficiently covered in cat spit, and speaking to us again, we made a thorough examination of his fur. He misinterpreted this action as cuddle time and purred up a storm. I didn't bother to correct him. Hubby couldn't find any fleas and declared Jasper safe and clean. Now that I'm recalling all this for your newsletter, it has just occurred to me that I never saw a flea in the first place. Hubby and I are going to have a little chat as soon as I hit 'Print' and put this week's adventure in an envelope to you.

JASPER THE MOUSER

Dear Jennifer,

Final Jasper tale. Hubby was working out in the garage one morning and spotted a little mouse moving along the corner where we store paint brushes and drop cloths. Those drop cloths were prime real estate for a mouse family. Mice give me the creeps and I consider their removal to be man's work, like mowing the yard and taking out the trash. And also vacuuming, dusting and laundry.

Hubby decided that it was time for Jasper to start earning his keep. Jasper had been practicing for years for this moment. He was very skillful at chasing laser lights across the room. He paid close attention to the spot where the laser light disappeared under the couch so that he could chase it when it came out again. Hubby didn't have the heart to tell him that he was turning the laser off at that point. Jasper might have paid us back in ways that weren't that funny.

Hubby took Jasper out to the garage and showed him his new workplace. Jasper had never been out there before. There was a lot of exploring to do. Interesting nooks and crannies were all over the place. Jasper's nose was on high alert. Hubby left him alone out there to do his cat thing and Hubby came back into the house to do hubby things (hopefully vacuuming, dusting and laundry). I was at the office and planned to remain there until my two guys took care of the vermin infestation.

After allowing several hours for Jasper to explore and get used to his new 'office', Hubby went out to check on things. I'm not sure what he expected to find, I mean, Jasper wasn't going to be holding up a sign that said "Got 'im." But what Hubby did NOT expect to find was Jasper resting casually on the hood of Hubby's car, flipping his tail up and down, checking his nails and looking bored. I'm pretty sure that Jasper considered mousing beneath him and he was not willing to get his feet dirty.

Wherever Jasper went when Life #9 was up, and whatever it is cats do there, I don't think he is catching mice. He is probably teaching the other cats how to say "NO" in any language, how to be wary of adults using baby talk, and how to be non-pourable in several different positions.

In the meantime, Hubby and I bought a bunch of mouse traps.

CAMPING MISHAPS

Dear Jennifer,

It's another exciting adventure in…Me when I'm not at the office…

Belle is 22 months old now and has expressed an interest in her potty chair. She has been observing bathroom behavior in others (those family members who don't scream if a little girl sticks her head in the room) and does a complete imitation of their motions; only she has no clue what she is doing, nor why she is doing it. This life's lesson prompted Bea to nag me about sharing my potty chair story with you. But after you read it, you must promise to chew up this paper and swallow it, so that no trace of my story gets out. And you must disavow any knowledge of the entirely true and unvarnished story you are about to read.

We used to camp in a pop-up when the girls were small. We loved our little camper. It was just the right size for weekend trips and getting the girls away from the television. One weekend we went to one of our state parks where the camp sites were very primitive. In case you aren't a camper that means there are no hookups – no electricity and no water. You're on your own. Bea was potty training and I brought her little chair with us to maintain a routine, and so she would learn that going to the potty is universal and occurs everywhere, not just at home. It was a nice potty chair, complete with arms and it folded up compactly for traveling.

Late that Saturday night I really had to go and it was quite dark outside. I certainly didn't want to trek all the way to the bath house and encounter a wild animal, like a bear or even a raccoon. Raccoons love campgrounds. They wait until everyone is asleep, and then raid the garbage cans. They get really testy if they feel threatened while they are eating old pizza crusts. I didn't know what I should do about getting the deed done. Everyone was asleep and if I were eaten by a bear I

11

wouldn't be missed until daylight. But wait! I had options! We had brought along Bea's potty chair, complete with arms! I considered myself rather slim, so I just sort of sat down on the little chair and did my thing. As I expected, I fit very well. As I had not expected, I fit too well and couldn't get up. My hips must have swelled during my stay, because they were oozing out the sides of those little potty chair arms. I never really knew I had hips until this moment.

Now I was in a predicament. I couldn't move much because it would risk splashing a pee pot all over a pop-up. Don't you just love alliteration? And I didn't want to wake the girls and have an instant audience. All that giggling would stress me and make me swell more, and maybe even alert other campers to the situation. Sometimes camping people are just a little too nice and helpful. They run to their campers for their tools and come back ready to help. I really didn't want a couple of good ole boys bringing over their channel grips and crowbars to assist at that moment. Hubby finally woke up and (in a loud whisper, so as not to wake the girls) wanted to know what was going on. Really? What does it look like? I have been taken hostage by a potty seat. He came over to assist and started working the potty seat off my rear end; much like you would struggle to get a size five ring off a size nine finger.

Somehow we got the job done without spilling anything. Hubby was a math major in college. He summed it up like this: my width was X and the chair's width was X/4. As nicely as he could, he asked me not to do that again. Ever. I had little square chair arm marks on my hips for two weeks. The girls slept through the entire episode, but their dad made sure to tell them the story, complete with embellishments. Bea grasped the concept of the story. But even with her limited 2-year-old's concept of getting stuck, spilling, etc., her dad has told it enough times over the years to fill any gaps in her understanding.

Before you chew up this paper and swallow it, sprinkle a little brown sugar on it first. It goes down easier.

THE DRIVE-IN RESTAURANT

Dear Jennifer,

I just love drive-in restaurants. They remind me of the 50s. What I mean is that they remind me of the drive-in restaurants from the 50s that my grandmother described to me.

We had dropped Ellen off at the Charlotte Douglas airport and she was on her way to Europe with her high school class. The rest of us were headed to the beach to drown our sorrows over one of us being so far from home for the first time. They say that our coastline is moving closer to our part of the state every year. If I can live another 50 million years, maybe I won't have to stay in the car so long someday. We had been riding in our Volvo station wagon for quite some time, so it's possible one or more of us were kind of cranky. Certainly not I, but Hubby and Bea needed a little attitude check.

Anyway, we were out in the middle of nowhere, and hungry, sad and a little out of sorts with each other. Also, my rear end was numb from sitting in the driver's seat for what seemed like the entire day. Bea was still too young to drive so she couldn't relieve me and I was too irritated with Hubby to let him help me (my martyr gene kicks in when I am aggravated). So there I was, a prisoner in the driver's seat and the sole decision maker of where we stopped to eat, not that there were any choices in the middle of nowhere. Miraculously, just as I was about to perish from starvation, one of those drive-in restaurants appeared on the horizon. I prayed that it wasn't a mirage. My last meal had been 4 whole hours before, and did I mention that I was thirsty?

We pulled up to a tiny, faded rusty intercom and tried to make our three-person order simple for the employees inside. We all wanted a burger, fries and drink. Nothing complicated. When you are near starvation, the simplest way is the quickest way. But the speaker wasn't working properly. Could I have just pulled away and parked at another spot with a working speaker? In hindsight, yes. But I was hungry, sad and a little out of sorts, so I stubbornly sat there, willing the intercom to work, and endured the painful aggravation. After all, I had been aggravated with my loved ones for several hours. Maybe I could take it out on a stranger for a while. The conversation with the person inside – it might have been an alien – went something like this:

Drive-In employee: Ma_I_ake__r__der? *static*
Me: I would like 3 burger meals, all with Coke.
Drive-In employee: D__u__ing__at? *static*

Hunh? I looked at Hubby. Normally, when I am hungry, sad and a little out of sorts, I would not flatter him by asking for his help; however, I wasn't stupid enough to think I could do this thing solo. He was still out of sorts, but he was beginning to get interested. This interest was probably driven by his own extreme hunger. He figured they were simply asking if we wanted everything on the burgers and offered his input, "Just say 'yes' to make it easier on everybody."

Me: Yes.
Drive-In employee: Do___w_nt___ke? *static*
I looked at Hubby, he nodded his head.
Me: Yes.
Drive-In employee: D_u__nt__a__? *static*
Me: Sure. Saying 'yes' was getting a little boring. I thought 'sure' might liven things up.
Drive-In employee:
__ay,__t's_ers___ies,__oke__be__en__inits. *static*
Me: Uh . . . okay.
Drive-In employee: $15.24. Thank you. *no static*

I turned to Hubby and remarked, "Well, at least the price was clear."

We were getting a little less out of sorts because the conversation had been somewhat entertaining and food was coming soon. My stomach was growling louder than I had been growling a few miles back. We actually started talking nice to each other again and even chuckled once or twice. Finally, all was forgiven and the conversation turned to the fun we would soon be having at the beach.

After a short wait, a teenage employee came out of the building with a tray and 3 buckets of drinks. We were sitting there wondering which car she was headed for and who could ever be that thirsty, when the girl approached our station wagon. Ours? We could never be that thirsty. It took me a minute to realize that all those gaps with static in the conversation were offers to bump up my order, which I did *every single time*. But now I know what 'Super-Size' means.

Our burgers and fries were very tasty, and they relieved those terrible hunger pains. But now about those Cokes. This all happened in the days before cup holders, (the days when you still had to crank your car window down by hand). Cup holders wouldn't have mattered anyway. We needed horse troughs to hold those cups.

Hubby put my drink on the floorboard between his feet. He was struggling to keep his own bucket of Coke from sloshing all over his lap. I have no idea what Bea was doing in the back seat, besides a lot of giggling. Caffeine does that to her. I had plenty of logistics problems going on in the front seat. If I was lucky enough to get stopped by a red light, Hubby would hand me my bucket of Coke with both hands, I would hold it with both hands, and drink what I could. Drinking from a bucket without carbonated liquid pouring out the sides and down all four of my chins was quite a struggle. I had flashbacks of my grandparents' farm, where Granny Lola fed Mabel the mule oats from a bucket the exact size as my Coke bucket. This brings up an entirely different topic: why did Papaw Herb name their mule after his sister-in-law?

Bea was so loaded with caffeine she didn't fall asleep until 4 nights later. I peed for an hour at a time for a solid week. Hubby has been hooked on Coke ever since that fateful night. Some nights I help him change his IV.

I am just now beginning to ask myself why we thought we had to totally consume all that Coke in the first place. Probably because I am cheap and I refuse to waste food, or let anyone else waste their food if they are sitting in my station wagon.

And that's my mostly true story with a moral: If you can't hear, don't assume, unless you are really, really thirsty.

A WEEK OF VACATION

Dear Jennifer,

I have been on vacation for the last week and a half and got to spend some extra time at the cabin. People are always asking us if we just sit around on the porch, sipping coffee and watching the river go by. Seriously? Who has time for that? It's a constant battle between us and Nature. Since we are only there on weekends and Nature is there 24/7, you can guess who is usually ahead in this contest.

Our latest battle has been the little scratching sound in the roof. The wildlife guy, Kevin, fixed that. He installed a little tool that allows the birds to leave but not return. He also found evidence of bats. Bats rate right up there with mice on my gross-me-out scale.

While Kevin was there we wanted to get full use of his services, so Hubby asked him about relocating our bobcat. This is the kind of bobcat that meows loudly and leaves heavy paw prints in our driveway, not the kind of bobcat that makes your overgrown yard look a lot better. Kevin went home for his bobcat trap and on the way back to our place he found a dead turkey, which really excited him, as this was free bait. I'm always amazed at what excites people. A dead turkey has never really excited me, unless it's plucked, roasted to golden perfection, and surrounded by mashed potatoes and gravy. I thought bobcats preferred their meals sort of…fresh. He explained that they do; the dead turkey would just rouse a little curiosity. So glad I'm not a bobcat. A lot of things make me curious: how do you pick out a good watermelon, how do 2 socks go in and only 1 sock comes out, where do all my pens go? Dead turkey – not on my list.

In addition to waiting for a bobcat we got a lot of gardening done. We are hoping to have a green bean tepee this summer and got that started. It wasn't too hard. When you have a zillion trees it is easy enough to find 12 little saplings to use as tepee poles. If it is successful I will send you a photo. If it isn't I will send you a picture of one you think is mine and let you brag on me. The massive herd of deer lingering at the edge of our woods is hoping it's successful. We also planted several rows of zinnias, marigolds, gladiolas and dahlias. I'm looking forward to seeing explosions of color in our flower beds over the next few weeks and months.

We came home on Sunday because the forecast was calling for rain in the coming days. If we are going to be rained in, it's always better to get rained in down here in town. The house is larger than the cabin and we can stay farther apart, a big secret to how we have remained happily married for so many years. And rain it did. I used my vacation time wisely by cleaning out closets, drawers, cabinets, and my side of the garage. I could start my own thrift shop now. I actually found Bea's baby album. Since she is child #2, you might not be surprised that most of the pages were still blank. So during my rainy vacation I worked on my 34-year-old baby's baby album.

We went back to the cabin the following Thursday after 10+ inches had already fallen in the mountains. My little flower seeds have probably washed all the way down to Cousin Junior's property which is 100 feet lower in elevation than ours. Maybe in a couple of months, he will let me pick my flowers from his yard. The river flooded again and washed away the plastic lawn chairs we donated to the family campground. Now they are somewhere between the campground and the Mississippi River.

The bobcat trap worked. It trapped a possum. You probably already know this but it is extremely difficult to reason with a possum. He/she was so stupidly happy in there, he/she refused to leave his/her comfy cage (if I can't tell the difference in kitten genders, there's no way I can get it right with possums). This was the comfy cage with a dead turkey in it and smelling pretty rank by this time. What sort of standards do possums set for 'comfy' anyway? It never occurred to that possum that he/she was sitting in a bobcat trap acting as live bait.

As clueless as the possum was, the bobcat was just the opposite. He knows a dead turkey trick when he sees one, so we have removed the cage and allowed the bobcat to roam freely around our woods, as long as he behaves himself and doesn't want to play cat and mouse with our little grandsweeties. (I could sort of tell what gender the bobcat is).

KUDZU

Dear Jennifer,

We are in the mountains this week and the other day we decided to try to get rid of some kudzu. I'm sure kudzu is no big deal in Chicago, but in the southeastern U.S., it is a curse. In case you don't know basic kudzu facts, I will give you a little background.

Kudzu is native to Japan and was introduced in the southeastern U.S. in the late 1800s as a means of controlling erosion. In Japan it grows like a normal plant, but here it can grow up to a foot per day. It sends out runners in all directions and those runners have new roots sprouting every foot, so kudzu multiplies quickly. The danger to plants is that the kudzu sends its shoots out, up and around and eventually smothers shrubs, trees, a team of horses, or whatever else is in its path. If you have ever driven through the country and noticed acres and acres of grotesque green shapes, those were innocent trees covered in kudzu. Some people have a thing about spiders or snakes. My thing is kudzu.

This afternoon I got kudzu fever and armed myself with a shovel, pickax, hand clippers, spade, hatchet, curved hand saw, and a little pointy pick. I made my poor husband come with me. He understands that it is easier to humor me than to try to reason with me on this subject. We were loaded for bear. Fortunately, we didn't see one of those. But we did find triple rows of rusty barbed wire. Accidentally. I forgot that my grandparents used to have cattle on that hill when it was pasture and not woods. It's a known kudzu hunter fact – when you are working on hilly terrain, in the woods, tripping over kudzu vines, rusty barbed wire fencing lies in wait to grab you right in the rear when you lose your balance. Thank goodness, no one will ever see THOSE scars. After an hour of chopping, digging and sweating, we unearthed 2 sizable root crowns. They were the size of basketballs. Basketballs with tentacles. They looked like wooden octopi. I was simply giddy with success. Score 2 for the kudzu fighters and 477,398 for the kudzu.

If you're lucky, I'll have another kudzu story later this summer. Maybe I will be able to tell you the one about the time I totally eradicated the big green monster. Seriously, the last thing I want is to retire to my cabin in the woods and sit in my rocker on the back porch staring at those hideous green shapes. I understand that kudzu is a salad green in Japan. I don't think I could look down in a salad bowl and see my worst enemy staring back at me.

POISON IVY

Dear Jennifer,

In all my years of suffering with poison ivy rashes, I never knew that there are levels of misery. If you brush against a poison ivy leaf, its oil will make the top layer of your skin extremely itchy for a week to ten days. BUT...if you are weed whacking and come in contact with the stem juice, it penetrates EVERY SINGLE LAYER of your skin and causes POWERFUL, IMMEASURABLE, INTENSE itching for a week to ten days. It bonds with the skin layers and behaves as a burn. I learned all this a week after whacking weeds (a week too late).

Basically, I have been suffering with 3rd degree itching for a week to ten days. Mine is always ten days. Show me someone who only gets it for a week. It was too hot to wear long pants and high boots that day while I was whacking away and now my lower legs and ankles are paying the price. I've been itching and twitching and we are completely out of steel wool. But there are some other items that relieve the itching when steel wool is not an option: coarse grit sandpaper and tree bark (now I know why bears scratch on trees).

It looks like I'm wearing red leather socks. Hideously ugly red leather socks. And I can't shave my legs without killing myself with the razor (no, the razor doesn't qualify as an itch reliever – it actually causes pain), so I look like a hairy ape. The poison ivy scrub I use removed all my tan (the expensive kind from a bottle), so I look like a hairy albino ape. A hairy albino ape wearing hideously ugly red leather socks. I had such a nice natural looking tan before I fell victim to the poison ivy scourge.

The other day Ellen brought the family up to the cabin and we went tubing on the river. As I approached the water disguised as a hairy albino ape wearing hideously ugly red leather socks, all the other tubers ran out of the river yelling "Leper! Leper!" Oh, please.

Poison ivy, in addition to being the bane of my existence, is also time released. That means that I haven't even started to suffer from my poison ivy exposure during last week's trek through the woods - this is just the weed whacking exposure from the week before. I might forget about the subject of this letter and complain all over again next week, so be prepared with tissues – it's going to be sad.

AGATHA AND ELMER

Dear Jennifer,

I haven't told you about Agatha and Elmer. Agatha was a 7th or 8th cousin on my mom's side and taught high school U.S. history for 107 years. She was a good U.S. history teacher, in part because she had lived through so much of it. She was also an impossibly hard U.S. history teacher, or so my older relatives thought. My great-grandmother sent word down through the generations to sign up for something easier than U.S. history, like the Justinian dynasty of the Byzantine Empire, so we wouldn't have to get a bad grade from her Cousin Agatha. Fortunately, Agatha was enjoying retirement when it was my turn for high school history, so I never had to suffer under her tutelage.

In the summertime, Agatha grew her own fruits and vegetables and often brought her canned goods to share at family reunions. The jars of pickled okra remained in the box in which they came, but we fought over her gooseberry jam. Agatha was married to Elmer, also a distant cousin somewhere up the line. In fact, after reviewing my family tree, which is rather tangled, I discovered that I am my own 12th cousin. But I digress.

Elmer probably didn't like that Agatha brought all the pickled okra back home from the reunion every year and none of the gooseberry jam. He was a rather cantankerous man – maybe because he hated okra. Nothing seemed to make him happy – maybe because he was married to Agatha. He didn't like the neighborhood kids walking on his grass, or the neighborhood pets sniffing around his yard. He fussed when the neighbor's leaves blew over the fence onto his side, and he fussed when his apple tree dropped apples on the neighbor's side of the fence. He became especially annoyed if that same neighbor ate one of the fallen apples. Elmer tried to set the right example for his neighbor by going over and collecting all his apples off the neighbor's grass and taking them back over to his side where those apples belonged. He wanted his neighbor to follow suit and come get his leaves.

Agatha and Elmer made a funny looking couple. Elmer was built like a pencil and Agatha was built like a Krispy Kreme doughnut. When they stood beside each other they looked like a 1O, which is not a score for perfection. Agatha was rather outspoken and knew how to throw her weight around. And she had a lot of it to throw. She was about 5'4". Both ways. And about half of that was rear end.

One fateful day, poor Elmer was taking an inventory of the apples on the other side of the fence when he passed on into Glory. Our family attended the funeral and the graveside service which followed. The old family cemetery was on a gently sloping hill tucked away in the beautiful Blue Ridge Mountains. It was a lovely and peaceful setting – most appropriate for launching a loved one off into his first chapter of Forever. It was even nice for Elmer.

The funeral home had set up 2 rows of folding metal chairs under the big tent for the family. A few neighbors (very few …okay 2) gathered around the edges of the tent. Most of the neighbors were back at Elmer's house, picking up free apples. To be brutally honest, it was surprising to see anyone at Elmer's funeral, including Agatha. Elmer had not encouraged many friendships in his lifetime, and from the lack of attendees that day his untimely death had not widened his circle of friends.

Agatha sat on the front row in the 'wife's chair' and their children (whom I had never met) filled up most of that row. I suppose they would have been my 8th or 9th cousins, but my family usually stops counting after 4. My sister Zuzu and I were on the 2nd row with the 'they don't matter much' kin. The minister began delivering his eulogy. He went on and on and on about what a wonderful, generous and kind man Elmer was. I checked the little bulletin they gave us to be sure I was sitting with the right group. Agatha sure got her money's worth out of this minister – if she paid him with something other than her pickled okra. He praised Elmer up one side and down the other so much that I began to believe Elmer was a great guy myself.

And then Zuzu got bored and stopped focusing on the minister. She looked around at the crowd, doing a little people watching (which didn't take long because there weren't very many people to watch), when she zeroed in on Agatha. Zuzu poked me in the ribs and whispered for me to follow her eyes and look this way …

Remember those folding metal chairs set up on the gently sloping hill? All of us mourners were facing uphill. As a person parks in a folding metal chair facing uphill, the body naturally wants to slide downhill toward the back of the chair. That is the natural direction when slick metal and gravity are working against the sitter. No problem for most of us. But Agatha was having a problem. The rear end half of Agatha wanted to keep going. That half reached the back of Agatha's folding slick metal chair but was not satisfied to wait there.

Did you ever see *The Blob*? Poor Elmer's cemetery scene was sort of like that movie. And poor Elmer's moment in the sun was being overshadowed by Agatha's rear end. It kept oozing out the back and over the sides of that folding metal chair and nobody could do a thing about it. And the minister kept going on and on and on about what a great man Elmer was. Maybe he was getting paid by the word. It probably didn't matter what he was saying by this time. Anyone not sitting in the first row of chairs was becoming more and more interested in the unfolding slick metal chair drama.

The situation was clearly getting out of hand. Or in this case, out of chair. And Zuzu was certainly no help. She got the silly giggles. Laughter is a wonderful gift. It makes the heart light and life worth living. It has healthful benefits. It is contagious. But sometimes it can be a real pain. Why is it that when you aren't supposed to laugh, everything is funnier? I was useless after that point. I bowed my head, praying that my trembling shoulders would indicate to the crowd ('crowd' might be a little too ambitious – let's say 'handful of bored people') that I was overcome with grief, praying that the minister would wrap it up, and praying that Agatha would be able to hold her head up after this incident. Remember the story about me wearing Bea's potty chair? This was like that, only about 200 pounds worse.

The minister finally said "Amen" and Zuzu made me sit there and wait for the chair to get up with Agatha. Obviously, this wasn't Agatha's first funeral on a hillside. She expertly wedged herself this way and that and managed to rise from her chair with poise and elegance. Most importantly, she rose without the slightest hint of discomfort and without the folding slick metal chair permanently stuck to her rear end. So impressive. And in uphill, gravity-defying form.

I wish she had been around when I needed to get out of that potty chair.

GRANDPA DANIEL

Dear Jennifer

Did I ever tell you about my Grandpa Daniel? Grandpa D. was quite a character. He had thick auburn hair until his 80s, something that made his 4 boys pretty jealous. In his 80s his thick auburn hair started to turn grey. I always thought his hair was due to his Scots-Irish background. I was told my whole life that Grandpa's branch of the family tree was Scots-Irish. Then I found out last year when I joined one of those roots websites, that all his ancestors were from Wales and England. I know my dad turned over in his grave right then. He was so proud of his Scottish roots. I'll have to check some of the other branches of our tree – maybe they won't disappoint.

But back to Grandpa. He was a farmer and raised tobacco, cows, chickens, peacocks, pigs and a horse named Duck. I never understood that last part. And the peacocks weren't on purpose; they just showed up one day, liked it there, and stayed. They dropped some gorgeous feathers which came in handy for decorating my room in the hippies era. Grandpa D. and Granny Carmen lived in a very small house back in the 'holler' and it was a pretty big deal when they got indoor plumbing. I was there. I remember doing things the other way up there. Their outhouse was a double seater and had plenty of old Sears catalogs on hand. It was parked over the creek and you could see the creek through the cracks in the floor – a pretty cool place to sit from October to May. The outhouse is still there. I wouldn't go in there now if you paid me. Goodness, I've gone soft.

But back to Grandpa. He was 19 when he married Granny, who was 15 at the time. Grandpa played the banjo and a Jew's harp. He let me try to play the Jew's harp once and I thought it would break all my teeth. Maybe I did it wrong or maybe the Jew's harp didn't bother his false teeth. In his wild and crazy days, he played his banjo on Saturday nights with some good ole boys in a barn somewhere. Think *Deliverance* with a boring ending.

When all the grandchildren were in, Grandpa would go into the house, push his upper plate out of his mouth about an inch, and come out on the porch growling like a monster with horrible teeth. It scared all my little cousins who ran screaming to their mamas, but I was the oldest, I had seen the denture trick many times, and I thought it was funny. Not very attractive, but funny. Grandpa was a heavy smoker, so those old dentures were not bright white like they are on those false teeth toothpaste ads. Grandpa also gave me my first cigarette. And my last. Every 8-year-old should be allowed to smoke a cigarette. It would save a lot more time and money than all those smoking cessation aids.

Grandpa D. wore faded denim overalls every day. On Sundays he wore his good denim overalls. I saw him in dress slacks only at funerals. My guess is that he only had one pair of dress slacks. My other guess is that he only had 2 pairs of denim overalls.

When he was younger (in his 60s) he would take Zuzu and me to the store up the road and buy us ice cream. That store is still there, only it sort of lists to one side now. Now I take my grandsweeties there for ice cream. What do they say about coming full circle? The real adventure was the ride in Grandpa's old truck. It seriously needed some new shocks. Maybe even *old* shocks would've helped. When he hit those bumps in the road, Zuzu and I would bounce so high, our heads would hit the ceiling of the truck. What fun! Seatbelts hadn't caught on yet. What a drag a seatbelt would be in Grandpa's old truck – there would be no adventure at all. I only told my dad about our adventures once, because I could tell right off he didn't like his dad bouncing us around the community in an old pickup truck. I didn't want to ruin a good thing.

Grandpa also had a taste for homemade liquor. There were lots of outbuildings around the farm – barns, woodsheds, a chicken house, a spring house, and a cellar, and he kept a little stash in each of those buildings, just in case he got thirsty. Granny wasn't aware of those quart jars all over the place because she spent most of her time in the garden and the house.

One day Grandpa picked up Zuzu and me to take us on his mountain version of a Disney ride and he stopped along the side of the road. He jumped out of his truck, reached behind the seat, and pulled out a quart jar. He had a swig, jumped back in the truck, and started again for the store. And he told us not to tell Granny. And we never did. We weren't stupid children. Those fun bumpy rides would have come to an abrupt end if we had blabbed our little secret. Grandpa's rides would also have come to an abrupt end after Granny got finished with him.

And that's just another twig on my tree that contributes to what makes me, well, me.

THE DRIVE THRU

Dear Jennifer,

One workday Hubby picked me up at the office for a quick lunch. To save time, we headed to our semi-favorite, one-star drive thru. You already know our history with giving orders through a speaker. This went no better. But Hubby was driving this time and I just sat back and observed. The order process went something like this:

Drive Thru person: May I take your order?
Hubby: Yes. I would like a cheeseburger with pickles and mustard (which is what I wanted) and a hamburger with ketchup, pickles, lettuce, and mustard.
Drive Thru person: That's a cheeseburger with pickles and mustard?
Hubby: Yes.
Drive Thru person: Do you want cheese on the other burger?
Hubby: No. Just ketchup, pickles, lettuce and mustard.
Drive Thru person: Okay. So on the second burger it's no cheese, just ketchup, pickles, mayonnaise and slaw?
Hubby: No. Just ketchup, pickles, lettuce and mustard.
Drive Thru person: Okay. Do you want cheese on that?
Hubby: No. Just ketchup, pickles, lettuce and mustard.
Drive Thru person: Okay. So on the second burger it's ketchup, chili, tomato and pickles?
Hubby: No. Ketchup, pickles, lettuce and mustard.
Drive Thru person: Okay. Do you want cheese on that?
Hubby: No. Just ketchup, pickles, lettuce and mustard.
Drive Thru person: Okay. So on the second burger it's ketchup, mustard and chili?
Hubby: Yes.
Drive Thru person: Do you want cheese on that?
Hubby: Sure.

Honestly, if he had continued his fight for what was right, we would still be sitting there. At least the girl got *my* order right. I had a really good cheeseburger with pickles and mustard, and some killer fries. They sure didn't get the fries wrong.

I have a theory about this lunch date. The drive thru person was one of Hubby's former math students who couldn't make an A in Algebra I. Maybe she couldn't make a B or C or D, either. She saw him coming from a mile away and decided to settle the score. It probably didn't happen that way, but there were no mistakes on *my* order, so we couldn't blame it on the intercom system. It was definitely on the part of the hearer. Hubby had to force down a cheeseburger that he hated and who knows what the final toppings were? My guess is that whatever the last offer was from the drive thru person, the outcome was not the same. Hubby, always the teacher, had to give the drive thru person a grade. She got an F with no chance for a make-up exam.

UNWELCOME GUEST

Dear Jennifer,

You know our cabin is surrounded by hundreds of acres of forest. We only own a small portion of that, but combined with all the land owned by our neighbors and family, it's very nice because it affords us privacy as well as beautiful views. It is also home to an assortment of wild animals. So far, we have spotted foxes, raccoons, skunks, deer (I think they are shipped in bulk from other states), a bobcat, mountain lion, and coyotes. As I have stated before, according to the book of Genesis, we have dominion over them and they should be afraid to bother us. For the most part they have obeyed the scriptures, although we can hear (and smell) them occasionally. I almost forgot the possum. We do have at least one stupid possum on the property somewhere. He is probably married and has a large family.

On Memorial Day weekend our friends came up to spend the holiday with us. We tried to show them a good time. The guys went tubing and hiking and we girls went shopping in town and hiking later. It was very relaxing and a lot of fun. I had a meal plan for the entire weekend, so we ate well. Hubby always helped with breakfast. He cooked a lot of it outside while I worked in the kitchen. We were a good team and there were no slip-ups like blackened toast or rubber eggs.

The weekend flew by and before we knew what was happening, it was Sunday morning already – departure day for our friends. They had a long trip ahead of them and wanted to get an early start. Hubby and I made sure they started out with a good breakfast. He cooked bacon and grits outside while I whipped up eggs inside. We enjoyed our last meal together and waved to them until their car was out of sight. There was very little clean-up to do (our friends are very tidy people), so Hubby and I relaxed around the cabin for the rest of the day. You know I was wearing my comfy pajamas and fluffy bunny bedroom shoes all day.

Late in the afternoon it was time to start thinking about our supper. I had left something out on the back porch and went out the kitchen door to retrieve it. But I never got whatever it was that I went after. Right there TEN FEET in front of me was a full grown black bear. Sniffing the grill. On our porch. He/she saw me and took off like a scalded dog. I didn't want to be close enough to verify the gender, nor was that foremost in my mind at the time. I was so shocked I forgot to be totally petrified. It was like being up close and personal with the back end of a black hairy Volkswagen. With claws. But it wasn't up close for long. That bear sure could run fast. I just stood there with my mouth hanging open. At last, I finally grasped the meaning of 'surreal'.

After my heart started back up again and I had the good sense to go inside and tell Hubby about all the excitement he had missed, we concluded that the bear had sniffed the bacon cooking outside that morning. How far can the scent of bacon travel? It makes you stop and think.

Since then, my big hairy VW friend (or a member of the family) has eaten my goldfinch feeder complete with seeds and feeder hardware. You don't think about bears eating plastic until it happens in your own yard. He/she has knocked the grill completely off the porch and caused it to land on its lid with the wheels spinning helplessly in the air. How the gas tank didn't rupture is beyond me. He/she discovered my hummingbird feeder, sucked it dry, and then fell over backwards, knocking a flower pot off a table and breaking it. It is terribly easy to track the movements of a curious bear on your porch.

What gives me comfort is knowing how shy this bear is. He/she was afraid of me on the porch that day, or maybe it was my pajama pants, or my fluffy bunny bedroom shoes. My entire ensemble was mismatched and this bear could've been sensitive about that sort of thing. Either way, this was a smart bear and understood the verse in Genesis that explains my dominion over him/her. I wish he/she would explain the scriptures to my cat.

DON'T BUG ME

Dear Jennifer,

Last week's reference to a black hairy VW reminded me of Ellen's first car – a little red VW bug. She felt pretty smart being able to change gears and the car was cute enough to serve as a guy magnet. Maybe it was a guy magnet because Ellen was so cute. Come to think of it, my old VW never served as a guy magnet for *me*.

One year around the week of Easter, Hubby and Bea were down at Myrtle Beach in our camper trailer. We had upgraded from a pop-up by this time (and the camper trailer had indoor facilities – not torture chairs). Ellen and I were planning to bring Ellen's friend Tracy, and Bea's friend Hannah to join them at the campground. A beach trip is more fun for everyone if each girl has her own buddy (and the parents get some time off). No, we were NOT planning to sleep all those girls in the camper – Ellen and Tracy were going to stay in a tent.

We left town with Ellen and Tracy in the VW (crammed full of stuff), and Hannah with me in my Volvo station wagon (crammed full of more stuff). It was a nice afternoon, the weather was pleasant, and Hannah and I were enjoying a nice chat. I was feeling pretty cool that a teenager was comfortable having a conversation of any kind with me. Occasionally, I glanced in my rearview mirror to check on Ellen.

As Hannah and I were talking, I made some sort of gesture with my hand, it caught the stem of my glasses, and they flew off into a floorboard somewhere. Time for mild panic. Hannah could only stare at me in shocked horror. I sensed that my glasses were on my side of the floorboard, but driving, leaning over from the driver's seat to find them, and not dying were all pretty hard to do at the same time. There wasn't much time to think about this as I was driving on a major U.S. highway at full speed wearing no corrective lenses. I told Hannah to grab the wheel and steer us over to the shoulder. While I was fishing in the floorboard and easing off the accelerator, Hannah was doing an awesome job of steering from the passenger seat, having had no driver training experience whatsoever. I felt pretty smug about being able to put my glasses on and decelerate a car at the same time. We got our little problem resolved and pulled back into traffic.

At this point I noticed that I was *not* noticing a little red VW in my rearview mirror. Hannah kept chatting and I slowed way down so that Ellen could catch up. With our delay, she should have been right on my bumper. I was creeping down a major highway doing 20 mph and no little VW was in sight. I had to interrupt Hannah's incredibly interesting story that I wasn't listening to, to inform her that we had to turn around at the next opportunity. We drove in the opposite direction for 20 miles before I saw my little girl, her friend Tracy, and the little VW parked on the side of the road. I had to drive another few miles to find a turn off so that I could come back and assist. This gave me a few minutes to compose myself, get my heart to move out of my stomach, and move back up north where it belonged.

I pulled up behind the girls and didn't see any signs of a crash. I said, "Thank You, Lord," very quietly (never let your kids see you panic), and then approached the girls for a run down. I tried to act cool and not grab them in a tight motherly embrace. But I might have done that anyway. The little trunk lid in the front had not been securely fastened and apparently, the wind had caught it and yanked it up, blocking Ellen's view of the road and slinging everything out of the little trunk. Those things in the trunk were important things, like the jack and other car paraphernalia. While Ellen and Tracy were waiting for me to notice that they weren't behind me, they were wisely spending their time running onto the highway to pick up important things, like the jack and other car paraphernalia. Thank You, Lord, that I didn't see them running in and out of traffic on a major U.S. highway.

I was so grateful that the girls were safe. Now, what to do?

The trunk lid was warped from its little brush with wind velocity, so it was absolutely not going to shut and latch securely. We certainly couldn't risk this happening to Ellen again. I was the only adult in the group which put me in charge. I didn't have a clue. It never dawned on me that we should just drive the 20 miles or so back home and forget the whole thing. I had 3 teenage girls waiting for me to figure out how to get us to the beach. I began to hatch a plan.

Fortunately, we were all wearing sneakers. I made each girl remove a shoe lace from one shoe. I did the same, so I had a good length of shoe string rope. I used this rope to securely fasten the trunk lid to the bumper. Thank You, Lord, that the bumper didn't fly off and we have something to anchor to.

Next, how to finish our trip? I couldn't let Ellen drive the VW – we were both too nervous for that. Since I was in charge, and not loving that at all, I decided that Ellen and I would have to trade places. You probably already know that VW gears don't change the same way as Volvo gears – different countries of origin and all that. Did I forget to tell you that my Volvo station wagon was NOT an automatic? What a time to give a crash course to a teenager on how to change Swedish gears. But Ellen was a smart girl and she learned quickly. That was a good thing because we were running out of options, not to mention daylight. I didn't have to ask Hannah to ride with Ellen. She practically dove headfirst into the back seat of the Volvo.

We began our trip again, only this time, I was driving at a reduced rate of speed. As little as I know about cars, I was smart enough to know that you can only depend on a shoe string rope so much. We made it off the U.S. highway and onto the 2-lane country roads. Every time I counted 10 or so cars behind me, I would pull over; Ellen would pull over, and let a bunch of angry, impatient drivers go by. Our 5-hour trip was turning into 7 hours. Hubby started getting anxious at the 5-hour mark so he called. Remember those old car phones that were about the size of a brick? I had one in my Volvo. So Hubby got to talk to Ellen and she filled him in on all the excitement he was missing. It was okay that I didn't have a cell phone that night. I was too busy watching traffic in front of me, pulling over for the traffic behind me, and praying that we could make it to Myrtle Beach on a shoestring.

Hubby met us at the grocery store a mile from the campground. He was quite relieved to see all of us. We laughed and talked for a few minutes, and then it was time for the final leg of our journey. He offered to drive the VW the rest of the way in for me. He has owned 17 VWs in his lifetime so he knew how to get to the campground in this car. But little Bug and I had been through a lot together, so I wanted to finish the race that had been set before me.

But I couldn't, because the VW wouldn't start. It was completely out of gas. What a perfect insult to injury tag-on to my story. Since Hubby wanted to help, I let him help me push the VW over to the gas pumps. I think little Bug had seen too many *Love Bug* movies and had decided to put on some attitude. In spite of everything, we all had a fun weekend, Hubby fixed Ellen's VW, and we got to add some funny notes to our Memory Jar at home. I think Tracy and Hannah were wise enough to keep their parents from finding out about their ride down to the beach. Otherwise, Ellen and Bea would've been friendless on future beach trips. I know I certainly wouldn't let *my* children ride in a car with a crazy lady who slings her glasses around and steals kids' shoelaces.

GRANNY'S GONE BATTY

Dear Jennifer,

Hubby went out to the shed for something the other day and a bat fell down at his feet. Let me just say that bats rate even higher on my gag-me meter than country music. Mice are a close second. Bats are creepy. They are mammals that fly, so that should be a sign that they can't be trusted. Bats land on your neck in the middle of the night and you wake up undead the next morning and stay undead for the rest of your life.

The reason I'm so anti bats is probably because hundreds of them took up residence in the attic of Granny Lola's old farmhouse. We lived with her for a while when my dad was transferred to that part of the state. Granny's old house had no heat except a giant woodstove in the kitchen, which she kept going all day every day all year long, even in the summer. Her kitchen must have reached 400° on July afternoons. It was comforting in January - not so much in July. She kept a big pot of water on it because she didn't have a water heater. The advantage of this was that she always had hot water available.

Her plumbing system was a single pipe running from an underground spring into her kitchen. Bath time was interesting. The house did have electricity - one outlet per room. Granny didn't like to waste money so she only used 40-watt bulbs. Her monthly electric bill was about $.28.

Doing homework at night was challenging. You really need to see the paper if you are planning to write. There are two reasons this didn't affect me academically: all my little classmates lived in old dim farmhouses and Granny's sister Mabel was my teacher, so she understood the challenges.

All this is totally irrelevant to my bat story; I just added it for interest. Basically, I lived in an old house with bats in the attic.

The first floor of Granny's house was half living room on the front and kitchen and dining room in the back. There was no hallway; we could just go from room to room in an endless loop. This information will come in handy as I tell you my true and unvarnished bat story.

One evening we were sitting in the enormous living room – I never did understand why Granny needed so much living room space, especially when there was only one lamp in the entire front half of the house, burning a 40-watt bulb – when a bat flew through. My mom screamed, scaring little Zuzu, Granny had to comfort her, and my dad ran to get work gloves. With his work gloves on, Dad attempted to catch the bat. This bat wasn't planning to get caught, so it wasn't sitting still. It was flying from the kitchen to the dining room to the enormous living room to the kitchen to the dining room…you get the picture. Dad was running right behind the bat with his hands up in the air, hoping to grab it before it did some damage, like smearing bat stuff on the walls or ceiling.

Dad ran past me about five times with his gloved hands in the air, hoping to catch this bat, and I guess his plan was to tire it out. I know my dad was tiring out, so at least part of his plan was working. I'm pretty sure that was the last time my dad ran anywhere. My mom was a useless heap in the kitchen floor, having switched from screaming to laughing hysterically as she watched Dad run circles around the house, and Granny was busy calming Zuzu, so I figured it was up to me to help my Dad. I held the kitchen door open. Somehow, the bat was smart enough to go through the kitchen door, out into the darkness, and probably back to its bat colony in Granny's attic.

A few nights later, we were all upstairs in bed and I could hear scratching in the walls. Granny yelled at me for trying to upset Zuzu, who probably qualified for psychiatric help by this time. As I was explaining to Granny that for once I was totally innocent of picking on my little sister, a bat *walked right out* into the room. Its wings were behind its back and it waddled around like a little man worrying over his tax return. I'm pretty sure this bat was rabid. Or maybe that was Dad's bat, still exhausted from the chase. In any case, I kept my neck covered.

Obviously, something had to be done, so in the next few days, my uncle installed that thing where the bats could fly out at night, but not get back in. We lived on a farm, so there was no shortage of outbuildings for them to move to. The barn had to be a lot more peaceful than that crazy house where most of the inhabitants were either laughing or screaming.

Back to the present. So now our shed has bats. There is never just one bat. Bats are groupies. I hope Hubby understands that the next time he needs me to run and fetch something from the shed, he is going to get a flat refusal. I have my neck to think of and I don't like having fangs where my eyeteeth are supposed to go.

SASQUATCH

Dear Jennifer,

Granny Lola had 12 siblings. The other grandparents had fewer than 12, but in total, there were more than enough aunts and uncles in our family. Plus, they all lived within tobacco juice spitting distance and they all knew each other, including the in-laws. Some of their names were rather odd, probably because they were remote mountain hicks and had never heard of really good names to give their children. Erp? You really wanted to name your kid Erp? Did you have a problem with heartburn when you were expecting him? The year my uncle Joe was born, there were 3 other Joes born to our large extended family. So for the next 85 years all the Joes were called by their first and middle names: Joe Allen, Joe Thomas, Joe Kenneth and Joe Bryan.

But I digress. There were so many in our family, there was never a shortage of playmates at family gatherings. I could choose the age, gender, IQ and hair color of any cousin I wanted to play with. I tried to choose the smart ones, although they were usually taken first, or they were busy helping the ladies set out food on those long saw horse tables. To this day I have some really bright cousins. Some are school teachers, company executives, policemen and medical professionals. The really, really bright ones were smart with their money and have retired. I have a cousin who is a politician. He doesn't speak to me. Maybe he was looking for the smarter cousins, also.

And then there's cousin Sasquatch. He is in a class all by himself.

We call him Sasquatch because he is huge. Not fat. Huge. He is tall, muscular and heavy. His upper arms are hams. I'm not talking about those sissy little hams in cans. I mean those enormous country hams that you rub down with salt, wrap in fabric, and hang from the wood shed rafters. When he played college football, Sasquatch was not issued shoulder pads. Nature provided them for him. Besides, the school didn't have any pads large enough to fit.

One day Sasquatch was fishing and a baby black bear waddled into the river. Now everybody on the planet knows the presence of a baby bear is an indication of the presence of a mama bear. Sasquatch knew this also. But when the mama bear saw him and growled her warning at him, did he heed that warning and run for the hills? Not Sasquatch. He growled back at her. Okay, so the mama bear backed away. Hopefully, Sasquatch learned from this experience for the next time he sees a baby bear in the river, but probably not. One of these days, his head is going to be on display in that mama bear's trophy room.

Sasquatch is a deputy sheriff. Don't mess with him or you are toast, meaning if he gives chase and catches you – and he *will* catch you – he will sit on you and you will be as flat as a piece of toast.

Sasquatch is really a big sweet teddy bear. He would give you the shirt off his back. And if he were to do that, your whole family could wear it together. He comes in mighty handy when we need a 500 pound stone moved from here to there. He just hoists it up on his shoulder and deposits it where it needs to go. I can't imagine what he could do to my short brittle body if I ever offended him. In case you are on social media, don't mention that you know Sasquatch. He might turn mama bear on me.

HECUBA AND KIN

Dear Jennifer,

My aunt Hecuba celebrated her 90th birthday this week. We took her on a sightseeing tour around some of her old childhood haunts, we drove through our pretty little mountain town to show her all the new stores and improvements, and then we treated her to a picnic lunch at the state park, which she really enjoyed. Turning 90 is not unusual in my family. Many of my kin have reached that age and gone way beyond. The remarkable thing about Auntie is that she knew it was her birthday, she knew her age, and she acted like she always does - like she is still 36. In fact, the next day she was planning to drive to NC State and visit her grandson who lives in a frat house. That is something I wouldn't do EVER, even at my young age (I can't see your face, Jennifer, but I know what kind of expression you are wearing right about now). Anyway, Auntie is fearless and undaunted by driving around a huge college campus. And she still acts young-ish, and makes for some very enjoyable company.

Not like her grandmother, my great-grandmother, Miss Eliza. We called her 'Little Granny' because she was 4'10" and made me feel tall. She was a fun person. She enjoyed reading Zane Grey westerns, telling jokes and teaching me to crochet. Then she hit 90, whereupon she went gaga. Normally shy and quiet, her 90th birthday released her inner wild child. At a large family gathering, she chased Hubby around the house (the house with the bats) trying to kiss him. Maybe if he had known her better, he might have acquiesced. But they had just met that day, so their relationship had not had time to progress to the kissing level. He finally escaped and I found him several hours later at a cousin's farm down the road. He was hiding in the granary loft, traumatized. Poor guy. Confidentially, if Little Granny had been 20 years old instead of 90, Hubby probably wouldn't have run away. He was probably just upset that he was only attractive to short little old ladies.

Then there was Grandpa D. He and Granny Carmen were roommates in a 'retirement center'. Seriously, a real retirement center doesn't smell like bath powder and pine cleaner. The residents get dressed and do fun things, like load up on the bus and go places. These people only went one place – the cafeteria – and in their bedroom shoes. This was simply 'The Home'. But Granny and Grandpa managed to get assigned together, they weren't slaving away on the farm, and they were quite relaxed and happy.

Then Grandpa hit 90. One evening a nurse came into their room to check on them and Grandpa was over on Granny's side of the room with his hands around her throat. He explained to the nurse that his wife was having trouble sleeping. I guess he was just trying to help her fall asleep. Forever. Granny was approaching 90 herself, but had given up her thought processes years before, so she really didn't know or care. She probably thought Grandpa was just giving her a hug.

Then there was Grandpa's dad, my great-grandpa Virgil. He was just plain mean years before he hit 90. When he entered the living room from the dining room, I exited the living room through the front door. I learned how to spot a mean old man at an early age – remember Elmer? But when he hit 90 and went to The Home, things got interesting. Grandpa D. went to check on him one day and saw Virgil and an ancient female inmate walking down the street, several blocks away from The Home. They were on their way to get married. How exciting to be old and in love without a care in the world. I guess the little girlfriend could see past great-grandpa's mean streak. Those wild, crazy kids.

Virgil's late wife, my great-grandmother Lulu, was sort of crazy all her life. Her parents must have known in advance and named her accordingly. Or maybe she was nuts because she was married to Virgil. Then she hit 90. Suddenly she started having conversations with the trees. Before, she only talked to her chickens. They sort of replied, making little clucking sounds, but trees can't really talk back. Perhaps since Virgil was her only source of an exchange of ideas, talking to the trees was more enlightening.

This does not bode well for me. I have some DNA to fight. But it looks like I have until I am 89 to start getting concerned. I have a feeling that Ellen and Bea will take me on a tour of The Home shortly before my 90th birthday.

.

NEIGHBORS

Dear Jennifer,

When Hubby and I were newlyweds we lived in an older established neighborhood full of sweet retirees. They treated us like their own children and we felt like much loved step-children. We had our favorites.

Miss Naomi was getting on in years and knew she shouldn't be driving anymore, so she put out the word that her late husband's old truck was for sale. It was one of those pickups with a wooden fence around the top of the bed to keep a cow from falling over the sides. We never knew her husband and weren't sure why he would have needed this sort of vehicle in town. Our town didn't allow livestock within the city limits. Naomi certainly didn't have any cows in her backyard.

A gentleman living a few streets over heard about the truck and sent word to Miss Naomi that he would like to have it. I think he showed up with $300 and Naomi was happy. She had always liked this guy, so she included a little bonus with his purchase. Her exact words were: "No charge for the new paint job". The buyer should've given the truck the once over before he let go of $300, because he was the new owner of an old truck covered with two fresh coats of sky blue house paint.

Miss Albertine lived across the street with her twin sister Miss Alberta. They were spinsters and dressed exactly alike all their lives. Although they were identical, it was easy to distinguish them. Miss Albertine was very active and outgoing and Miss Alberta was quiet and liked to keep to herself. They were both gems. Miss Alberta baked goodies and Miss Albertine delivered them.

Hubby and I were often the grateful recipients of a plate of goodies – brownies, cookies, always something bad for our teeth. How I miss those visits. Miss Albertine always stayed for a brief chat and then left to check on her other neighbors.

Conversations with her were never very stimulating. We let her do most of the talking. Albertine always worried about poor old Alberta who repeated herself a lot. And a couple of sentences later, she mentioned poor old Alberta who repeated herself a lot. And after another 5 minutes she brought up poor old Alberta who repeated herself a lot. I just smiled and acted like I was listening. And I would never hurt her feelings, so it would be impossible for me to let on that she was much worse than poor Alberta.

In order to include Miss Alberta in conversation, I always tried to return the empty cookie plate while her sister was out making her rounds. This was best accomplished by emptying the cookie plate into my own container just after Miss Albertine left our house. Then I had plenty of time to return the clean plate to Miss Alberta and have a quiet little chat with her. She often worried about her poor sister who repeated herself a lot. Bless their hearts.

One summer the twins invited us to join their family reunion down in the country. This was a great plan for all involved. Hubby and I were young and poor and this was a golden opportunity for a free meal. The twins knew that Hubby would offer to drive and they wouldn't have to – a perfect win-win.

Our instructions were to be ready to leave our street at 11:30 a.m. to allow plenty of time for our drive to the country, arrive at the old homestead, and visit with family until the meal which was scheduled for 1:00. On the morning of the big day, Miss Albertine was at our house at 10:30 in a snit, and with food containers in her arms. We had to leave RIGHT THEN. A cousin had decided that he couldn't wait until 1:00 to eat so he was moving the mealtime back somewhat. He must never have heard of 'snacks'. The ladies were stressing because this was NOT according to plan. Fortunately, all the dishes and goodies had been prepared the night before. We loaded the food in our car and left. The twins were in the backseat not speaking. Not even Miss Albertine who was *never* not speaking. I tried a few times to make conversation, but I was met by 2 sets of puckered lips. Those girls were miffed.

We arrived at the homestead with several other family members, all of whom were running from their vehicles to get food on the tables. The twins took their casseroles into the kitchen to do some last minute prepping and warming up. There was a long line waiting for the oven because many cousins had been caught off guard by the sudden time change. All were jockeying for position to get their food finished and out the door to the tables. Microwaves weren't around yet. I was feeling very smart to have contributed sweet tea and deviled eggs. You don't have to wait in line to get those items ready.

This cousin who changed the plans must have been The Alpha Cousin. Nobody in *my* family moves that fast when a cousin issues an order. Overall, the twins had a lovely family and everyone was polite to us and kept checking to see if we had enough to eat. Hubby and I had enough to eat. We didn't have to eat again for another 3 days. We never got to meet The Alpha Cousin. According to all the sources on Proper Etiquette, the twins should have introduced us to this important person, but they were sitting off to themselves with their lips still puckered. It must have been very difficult to eat fried chicken and chocolate pound cake with their lips drawn up like that.

STICKY THANKSGIVING

Dear Jennifer,

I love Thanksgiving. It is my absolute favorite holiday. There is no stress about buying gifts, or fighting traffic. The only traffic is in the grocery store - the stuffing aisle and the checkout. And there is a little stress around the waistband if you taste everything to avoid offending anyone who brings food. That is the real reason I always have 3 desserts. It's not because I love dessert. I am simply being politically correct. I also know to wear stretchy pants on Thanksgiving Day.

When the girls were teenagers we had 2 groups of family over for Thanksgiving meals. One group came at lunchtime for the beautiful turkey. The other group came for dinner and we combined leftovers, which was a lot of fun.

One year Family Group 1 came for Thanksgiving lunch. I had spent the week before decorating the tables with pretty tablecloths and centerpieces made of cornucopia, silk leaves and votive candles. In the dining room I had fashioned a fall wreath around the brass chandelier. It is out of style now, but I am too cheap to replace it. But that Thanksgiving it was really pretty and still in style. My best tablecloth was on the dining room table that my parents bought in 1968. You probably don't ever want to see my eclectic collection of furniture and décor. Most days, I don't even like to look at it.

We had a nice time together, and then Family Group 1 left early in the afternoon. That gave us just enough time to clean up, set up for Family Group 2, and grab a quick nap. All that eating can certainly wear a person out. We took a quick nap, relit the votive candles, and started heating up leftovers for the 2nd shift.

Our family has always had a tradition of inviting someone who might not have a family to celebrate with. We hate thinking that someone we know might be alone on

Thanksgiving Day. This particular year my new son-in-law Jarrod was planning to bring his grandfather to our evening meal. He was a very distinguished man and I always enjoyed talking with him.

As I was heating up leftovers in the kitchen the second shift began arriving. I was beginning to make another pitcher of sweet tea. I had a cup of sugar in the tea pitcher and had added a quart of cold water to it. I use a tea maker so the other quart of water was going to get heated up and shoot out into the container holding the tea bags. But I didn't get that far into the process. Just as I was pouring water into the tea maker, my sister-in-law was entering the front door yelling that the dining room table was on fire. That is a phrase you don't want shouted in your house on Thanksgiving evening.

I don't react to tragedy well, so I grabbed the first fire extinguisher I could think of, which was a quart of cold water with a cup of sugar in it. I ran with it into the dining room where I saw a small campfire burning on top of my 1968 table. Thank goodness my aim was good. I only had the single quart of water to do the job. I certainly couldn't tell that little fire to hang on a minute while I ran back for more water. Fortunately, it was a small fire and didn't do any real damage, except to my best tablecloth and all those pretty silk leaves. Silk leaves don't burn well. They sort of turn into tar. And although the flames didn't amount to much, the smoke more than made up for it. My pretty wreath around the chandelier was a crispy black stick. My best tablecloth had a burned-out hole in the very center. Hubby picked up all four corners of the tablecloth and carried it, my dead silk leaves, my dead cornucopia and my dead votives, which started the whole thing, out to the yard and left them there. How embarrassing. There's a little sticker on the bottom of the votives: burn within sight. They really weren't kidding when they printed that sticker.

Next on the agenda: clean up detail. Do you know how long it takes to get a quart of sugar water wiped off the floor and rug? In some cases, several weeks. It took that long before our shoes stopped making a little 'thck, thck, thck' sound whenever we walked by. We would grab a wet paper towel, wipe down that area, think we finally had all the spots wiped clean, then hear 'thck, thck, thck' again next time we walked by.

We managed to get everything settled enough to enjoy our Thanksgiving leftovers. Jarrod's grandfather never said a word during the entire episode, but as he was leaving, he thanked me for a delicious meal and noted that Jarrod's new family sure is an exciting group.

He never visited our house again.

FUN AT WORK DAY

Dear Jennifer,

I wish you had not been traveling on Fun at Work Day. It was a lot of fun and you would have enjoyed it immensely.

I was a little skeptical. The snacks weren't a problem. Snacks are never a problem. Neither is joining Weight Watchers.

Anyway, Judy forced me to play checkers with her. I stink at checkers. Judy does, too. I wiped up the floor with her. Then I was peer pressured into playing corn hole. This is a good spot to tell you that in elementary school I was always the last one chosen for the softball team, probably because if the ball ever came close to my location way out there in left field, I covered my head. If I was at bat, I hit the catcher instead of the ball. In my defense, the catcher was an easier target than that tiny little ball. In junior high school there were five field hockey teams in P.E. class: Excellent, Good, Fair, Poor and Moron. My P.E. teacher assigned me to the Moron team. Her goal was to make me feel disgraced and become athletic overnight so I could graduate from Moron to Good. This ploy worked on the smartest girl in school. She also started out as a fellow Moron, but she was used to being the best and fought her way up through the ranks over the course of our field hockey study. The oblivious P.E. teacher didn't know me very well. I didn't care enough about field hockey to even fight my way up to Poor. Zits, Algebra, and crushes on cute boys were all I could juggle at one time. She tried every trick in the P.E. teacher's manual to shame me out of my Moron status. If times had been different, my dad could have sued that teacher for my emotional pain and suffering, and I could have owned every pair of sweat pants she had.

But I digress. I had to play corn hole with my coworkers. Since my P.E. teacher wasn't around – she's probably 110 years old by now – I didn't feel a lot of stress, but I was waiting for my turn and wishing I could be working at my desk instead of having all this fun. Brent was my partner because Delilah and Anita are extremely competitive and they promised to stuff me down the elevator shaft if I made them lose. Not really, but I can read body language.

And guess what? I scored 3 points. Not only that – my team won. Not bad for the lowest ranking member of the field hockey Moron team.

But the best part was the jigsaw puzzle area. That's my kind of sport. We have all decided – those of us who like jigsaw puzzles – to make it a permanent 4th floor activity. Those things are a very good outlet for getting your mind off fabric and trims for a few minutes. For the record, I rated Excellent in jigsaw puzzling. Not Moron.

SNOWY DRIVEWAY

Dear Jennifer,

Last Friday night, the snow was getting serious as we arrived at the cabin. There was already about an inch on the ground. When your driveway is steep and curved and your truck has sissy tires, it can get serious quickly. Years ago, before we built the cabin, we just had a camper trailer and an old shed on the property.

Late one autumn we needed some extra space in the garage and thought we could really use the space our generator was taking up. We hadn't needed it for a couple of years and we could easily store it in the old shed in the mountains. We took it with us on our next trip up.

Isn't life funny? Exactly two months after we moved the generator our town had a record-breaking ice storm. Electric lines were down all over the area and the power company couldn't promise anything within the next few days. The generator was up there and we needed it down here. Hubby wanted to go to the hardware store and buy a generator. You know I'm cheap. I reminded him that we already had a perfectly good generator in the mountains, and I had a feeling there were no available generators within a hundred mile radius. We'll never know about that part. So we got ready for a trip up the mountain.

Bea was still a kid so we made her go with us. She was ready for an adventure anyway. We had more of an adventure than I bargained for, which is usually the case.

Part one of our adventure was just getting ready to go. We owned a 1973 International Scout. It had been a much loved machine over the years. I would like to have known its history. It looked like it had had some wild times. By the time it was ours it was held together with some solder and duct tape and covered with camouflage paint. The windows didn't go all the way up and to ride in it without suffering too much, we had to wear several layers. We put on all the clothes we owned, packed some snacks and headed out.

The first two hours of our drive were rather treacherous. Sleet was still falling and coating everything, including the roads. Once we reached a certain elevation the ice stopped and changed to snow. Things began to look promising. Then we reached our property. The property that sits on a one lane road that the snow plows eventually get to after the important roads have been scraped. They had not gotten to our road yet. And there were twenty inches of snow on our driveway. It was really pretty, though.

The good news was that our International Scout was built for just this type of trouble. Hubby started up our steep, curved driveway. We were about a third of the way up when we started sliding. You might be interested to know that I can hold my breath for a full three minutes when I'm terrified.

Hubby turned to me and told me quietly to get Bea out and walk with her the rest of the way up. You must be joking. It's dark and icy cold out there. (Technically, with the windows not completely closed, it was dark and icy cold inside the vehicle anyway). Why do you get to drive and we have to walk? Did I offend you in some way? No, he was afraid the Scout was going to slide off the driveway and didn't want all three of us to plunge to our deaths together. Isn't that sweet? We wouldn't have died together but we could have died close to the same time. He would have plunged to his death in the Scout and Bea and I would have frozen to death in the shed. It was 10° outside, so I'm pretty sure I'm right about that part. We didn't have cell phones yet, so it wasn't like I could have dialed 911. It was too far to walk to Cousin Ambrose's house. He would have discovered an ice sculpture in the shape of me along the roadside when he left home the next morning. These thoughts were running through my head as I considered all the possibilities. *All* the possibilities? There were none.

Bea and I plodded uphill through the snow and made it to the shed where the generator was stored. I may have suffered frostbite. My toes were so cold I couldn't tell. Hubby arrived within a few minutes, still driving the old Scout. For the record, I can outrun a 1973 Scout going uphill, in the dark, and in adverse weather conditions.

I wasn't very helpful from that point on, not that I had been too helpful before. My fingers had turned to wood and it was difficult to wrap them around anything on the generator that would enable me to help lift it into the Scout. Bea was just a little kid so we made her stay in the vehicle. Kids are so lucky.

Do you know how much a generator weighs? More than I can pick up, that's how much. Fortunately, I was motivated by the fear of freezing to death and reached down into the depths of my being and told myself to buck up and get moving. By the grace of God we finally got that generator loaded. Maybe I should have prayed in the first place.

Then it was just a matter of locking up the shed and starting back down the driveway. This time I was praying that we would make it safely down the hill and that Bea and I wouldn't have to get out and walk again. Walking with wooden toes is very difficult. The Scout slipped and slid all the way down the driveway – I'm pretty sure the driveway was a mile long that night, although it is a lot shorter than that now – and made it safely to the bottom, thank the Lord.

After that, we faced the problem of going back down the mountain in falling snow. We were 30 miles from the old shed when we came upon a barricade across the road. A tractor trailer had slid off the side in a curve and was half on-half off. The tractor portion was over the side, looking down a steep embankment. Hubby had to do a 15-point road turn to get us pointed back up the way we had come from so that we could find an alternate route home. I wanted my mama.

The first thing I did when we got home was to call Mom and tell her about our exciting evening. She thanked me profusely for not telling her ahead of time and making her worry about our safety. I'm a pretty good daughter about stuff like that. The next thing we did was to set up that generator and make it worth our trip. I was so glad that Hubby is always prepared and had plenty of fuel to get it up and running. I was so grateful to be back home, safe and warm, I never once complained about the deafening noise those generators put out.

As it turned out, our trip paid off. We were without power for nine days. That storm and subsequent loss of power made me grateful for lamps, and running water, and hair dryers, and furnaces, and refrigerators, and electric blankets, and toasters, and water heaters, and...

SISSY TRUCK

Dear Jennifer,

We thought it would be a fun adventure to spend another cozy weekend snowed in at the cabin so we took off after work Friday and headed up there. We saw some beautiful scenery along the way and expected some awesome views from our back porch. The days are so short now it was already dark by the time we reached our property.

The good news was that the snow plows had already been down our one lane road. The bad news was that they had pushed up a mountain of snow along the edge of our driveway, completely blocking access. More bad news was that the mountain of snow was over three feet high, we hadn't brought a shovel along, and we were in a sissy truck. It's times like this that I miss that old Scout.

But I am married to a genius. Hubby started driving back and forth over the snow mountain, just a tire width at a time and eventually mashed the entire barricade down to a reasonable depth. Then it was a simple matter to start up the driveway, unlock the gate and keep going. That was the plan, alright.

The plan didn't work. The truck didn't even make it to the gate. Sissy tires. I offered to jump out and unlock the gate so that chore would be out of the way. Why didn't it occur to me that I had left home in tennis shoes? I jumped right into two feet of snow. Snow down in your tennis shoes is most uncomfortable. Snow shoved up your jeans legs isn't much better. But I have a bit of the martyr in me, so I unlocked the gate anyway and secured it. Hubby came up beside me and saw the results of my poor selection of attire. He is almost always prepared (he didn't pack a shovel, so I can't truthfully say that he is *always* prepared) so he got out his extra boots for me to wear.

Wasn't that sweet? He wears a size 11 and my shoe size is 7. I felt like Hans Christian Andersen's *The Little Match Girl*. Remember her ill-fitting shoes? She didn't make it. I planned to survive. Now that I had serviceable footwear, we moved on to Plan B for getting up the hill.

Hubby thought driving at a high rate of speed would get the truck up the driveway so fast, he would be at the top before the truck realized what had happened. I watched him backing down the one lane road completely out of sight. I don't know how far he went, or what he was expecting to do if another vehicle came along, but suddenly I heard the roaring of a truck engine and saw a big red pickup truck racing toward me. At this time it seemed like a good idea to stand behind the gate for added safety.

Hubby came tearing up the driveway and came to a dead stop about fifteen feet past the gate. This looked like a good time for a Plan C.

Plan C was basically DIY. We had a cooler, groceries, a very important purse, Hubby's laptop, and other extremely necessary items that we required in the cabin. Our first idea was to carry the cooler between us, each holding a handle. There were two problems with this: Hubby's stride is much longer than mine and I was wearing a pair of men's shoes. I was wearing a pair of men's shoes that remained in the deep snow every time I lifted my foot to take another step. I was extremely frustrated, but couldn't cry because my tear ducts were frozen.

We decided to split the load. Hubby was able to pick up the cooler and carry it and I grabbed all the stuff I could reasonably carry. Naturally, Hubby made better progress than I. He was wearing shoes that fit his own feet. I was forced to stop between steps and pick up each foot out of the snow while still holding onto all that stuff I thought I could reasonably carry. Then something wonderful happened. Sasquatch had been hunting on our property and I discovered the big footprints he had left behind. I was never so grateful for footprints. I was able to step in them which made climbing our steep driveway in deep snow a little easier. Not a lot easier – I was still wearing men's boots – but somewhat easier. We managed to make it to the cabin and get inside. I was grateful for many things that night, one of which was a pair of boots my size in the closet.

But first, we just sat down and breathed for a few minutes. What a nice recliner we have! What soft rugs on the floor! What a warm fireplace! Aren't gas logs wonderful? After a brief rest, we put on items of outdoor clothing that fit; we grabbed a couple of flashlights, and headed all the way back down the driveway in deep snow for another load. The next load wasn't nearly so bad. It's amazing what wearing your own size shoe can do for your outlook.

The moon was out and helped us stay on the path instead of stepping off into thin air. Stepping off into thin air on a cold snowy night can put a real damper on your evening. We got all our supplies up to the cabin and left that sissy truck down at the gate for the rest of the night. In all, it took us as long to finally get from the gate to the cabin as it did to get to the mountains from our house. What an evening! Next time we want an adventure, we should probably be a little more specific about what sort of adventure we have in mind.

THE EARLY YEARS

Dear Jennifer,

My dad's job transferred us around the western part of NC every few months until I was 11 years old. I learned that there are many varieties of Southern accents and mannerisms, which I had to adopt in each new location in order to be accepted by my little peers. The cliques were established by the time I arrived in the area and being clique-less is pretty tough on a little kid.

I was the new kid in class every semester from grades 1 – 5 (fortunately, public kindergarten wasn't invented in our state yet, or I would've been forced to add another clique to my collection). Since I was the oldest grandchild on both sides and both sides lived within a mile of each other, I was used to being the center of the universe and the darling of all gatherings. What an unpleasant surprise to walk into a classroom full of strangers for the first time and not be immediately loved, appreciated, and showered with hugs and kisses.

I was almost always blessed with a sweet, understanding teacher who knew I was terrified and wanted to make a U-turn and go straight back home to my mama. Almost always. There were a couple of teachers who did not recognize nor appreciate my darling status and actually treated me as a regular kid.

In one of my second grade classes we were drawing trains one day and my teacher blasted me in front of the class, telling me that my locomotive was too big and too black. Well, I just have to ask: what is bigger and blacker than a locomotive? But it got worse. She grabbed my hand and marched me down to the first grade hall to show me their properly drawn and softly colored locomotives. Who knew black could be considered a pastel? How humiliating - to be shown up by a group of first graders. But she eventually redeemed herself when she started appreciating my darling personality and made me the official teacher's pet. It certainly took a lot of work on my part to get to darling status with her, though. Very tough job with only five months in which to get it done. You can guess that the darling status was short lived. It was on to a new town, new clique and another new teacher challenge soon afterward.

One of my fourth grade teachers plopped me down in the back of the room in a wooden desk designed for a left-handed student. I learned early on that when you're the last one in, you get the leftovers. I informed her that I wasn't left-handed and she told me to deal with it. Excuse me? You must not realize that I am a darling. And I may have known I was a darling, but I was also very shy, so when she told me to deal with it I dealt with it. She and I never did reach the darling level together.

Things started smoothing out when the state allowed my dad to hang around the same town for the remaining years of his employment. What a strange experience: visiting the same dentist twice.

But then junior high struck. My first experience with changing classes, changing buildings and changing clothes in front of everybody in P.E. How painful. And my P.E. teacher hated me. I know this because every time she looked at me she rolled her eyes and 'hrumphed'. There's nothing that says 'I hate you' like an eye roll followed by a 'hrumph'. It was okay, though. I didn't like her, either. Not only was I not at darling status with her; I couldn't even get above moron status (not that I made any attempt at it). You know my sorrowful moron story. You probably thought I was exaggerating. Sorry - no. Unfortunately, she was my P.E. teacher for 3 long miserable junior high years. We did agree on one thing: we both looked forward to the day when I would move on to high school. Zuzu had this same teacher when it was her turn for junior high P.E. and the teacher asked her if I was still a klutz. Well … kind of. I said I was a darling. I never said I was a *graceful* darling.

SKINKY HAIR

Dear Jennifer,

I haven't shared a weird animal story with you lately and I know you have missed it, so here is another true, hardly embellished animal tale straight from the Family Vault of Weird Things:

A few years ago we had to be at church on a Sunday afternoon to set up for Vacation Bible School. We parked the Volvo wagon in the shade and headed for the basement door. Something tapped the top of my head and I was dismayed to think that I was the victim of a bird bomb in the church parking lot. I had no time to go back home and make repairs and there certainly wasn't any equipment at church. Ours was a small family church and didn't have shampoo, conditioner, mousse, hair dryer, styling brushes, or spray in the janitor's closet.

The girls and I went inside and were greeted warmly by those who had arrived ahead of us. One of the teenage boys came up to say 'hello', and since he was taller and could see the top of my head, I asked him to assess the damage back there. He was happy to help. We were always close like that.

His sweet smiling face changed to a look of abject horror. "There is a lizard in your hair!" he screamed. Well, that certainly got everyone's attention. One screamer in a church basement is enough, so I calmly said, "Then, someone get it out."

And he did, or he tried to. The little reptile on my head was not in a mood to be caught, so he made a leap to the floor. That was fine with me, but my teenage friend felt it was his duty to rid the church basement of this evil beast. I saw the little guy and it wasn't a lizard, but a skink. It may surprise you to know that spiders and reptiles don't bother me that much, in fact, skinks are kind of cute. I just don't particularly care for one in my hair. If a bat or mouse had been in my hair, I would still be in a catatonic state.

We have always had little skinks hanging around our house. They seem to like our bricks. I may have even brought this little guy from home. I hope not, because I didn't get to take him back to his family that day, which was really his fault since he ran off. I wrote a limerick to mark this event:

There was a small reptile, I think
That might have been known as a skink.
He liked my brown hair,
And so he stayed there.
At least he didn't make my hair stink.

OUR FIRST TREE

Dear Jennifer,

What do you think of our Christmas décor at the office? My tree at home finally has ornaments on it. Twelve in all. I just can't bring myself to dig all those ornaments out of all those boxes. The tree might stay at a twelve ornament limit for the entire Christmas season.

Our first tree was pitiful. I was in college and Hubby had his first job out of college. Our yearly salary was less than what I paid for groceries last month. So when it was time to get a Christmas tree, we went to Hubby's grandpa's farm and got a freebie. It was really cute and had a nice shape. It was the right size and looked almost like those expensive trees on the lot. We had just enough money to buy a box of those red satin covered balls. One box. Twelve ornaments. Maybe I'm on a theme here with the number twelve.

We put those ornaments on the tree and thought it was the prettiest thing ever. The wrapped gifts went under and we felt like grownups. Now usually, right about here in my letter, the weird part happens. Well, it's time for that now.

We positioned our little free tree in front of the picture window in the living room, right in front of a heat vent. Our tree and few wrapped gifts looked so festive for a day or two. Then the tree gradually started dripping sap all over our twelve red satin balls, and the wrapped presents. Then the heat came on. And when the heat warmed up our little free tree, millions of little aphids began to hatch. Those little aphids stuck to the sap on our twelve red satin balls and the sap on the wrapped presents. Now we know why Christmas tree farmers spray their trees so thoroughly.

We had to unwrap all the gifts. Aphids were stuck to the bows, the ribbons, and the gifts inside the wrapping. I can't explain how they managed to do that. It was disgusting. Fortunately, I had enough leftover gift wrap to re-wrap the gifts. My mother-in-law felt sorry for us, so she bought us a little artificial tree at Sears. Artificial trees are not prone to sap or aphids. And it was just as cute as Grandpa's little tree. With every gift we gave that year, we had to offer an explanation about the dead bugs stuck to the sap on the box. How embarrassing.

Over the years we have had many Christmas trees, but we always kept my mother-in-law's gifted tree. The girls put it in their playroom and decorated it with their own ornaments every year. We kept it until Bea went to grad school and took it with her to her first apartment. It might still be hanging around somewhere.

Dredging up these old sappy aphid memories is beginning to give me flashbacks. I think I'll go dig all those ornaments out of all those boxes and start decorating our tree. And I might spray it down with some bug spray. I don't care if it is an artificial tree – I don't want to take any chances.

BOWL ME OVER

Dear Jennifer,

Before you think I am terrible at every single sporting activity
I ever attempted, I must tell you that in college I did slightly
better. Maybe it took that long for my body to catch up with
my feet. My first college P.E. experience was tennis. My serve
wasn't bad, I actually managed to return the ball, and it
actually went over the net most of the time. In high school
tennis the ball went right over the chain link fence and it was
20 feet high. Our punishment for hitting the ball over the fence
was to go fetch. Just beyond the fence was a steep hill covered
with poison ivy. I had to go fetch a lot. I itched a lot, too.

But back to college tennis. Hubby took me to the park to play
tennis sometimes for practice. My final grade was a B. This
was like the Cinderella team winning the NCAA basketball
championship. I felt dishonest. I had to find my tennis
instructor to make sure she knew who she gave this B to. She
was so cute. Every day she wore white tennis socks with a
little fuzzy ball at the back of the foot. Every day her socks
had a different color fuzzy ball, so I know she changed her
socks every morning. Sorry, I didn't mean to get distracted by
socks. Anyway, I asked if her intent was to give me a B and if
so, why? Her answer was 'Yes' and that the name of the
course was 'Beginning Tennis' and I certainly played tennis
like a beginner. Too logical to argue with that, so I accepted
the B without any more guilt.

The next semester was bowling. I diligently applied myself to
the proper approach as I let go of the bowling ball. Right hand
supporting the ball against my chest with fingers applied just
so, left hand assisting the right hand. Step left, begin gradual
swing of the ball to the back, step right, ball should be behind
me, step left and release. It went in the gutter a lot. Once I
overheard my bowling instructor whisper, "Her technique is
perfect. I can't understand why she misses the pins." I
determined to improve to at least Fair status. She was so kind I

had to help her feel like a successful teacher. Hubby took me bowling sometimes for practice. I did meet my goal of Fair by the end of the semester.

Several years later some friends wanted us to go bowling. It had been years and years since I had visited a bowling lane, and I thought it would be more exciting to stay home and sort my spices in alphabetical order. But I went along to be nice. We got to the bowling facility and I picked out my shoes. I had my own bowling shoes in college. Why didn't I keep them so I wouldn't have to wear a pair of shoes worn by strangers? I had some difficulty finding a 10-pound ball. Anything heavier would have made my right arm longer than my left.

We started bowling and I bowled like I always did – Fair. There was a men's league bowling in the lane beside us. This was a serious group of men and they were all large guys. They were built a lot like Fred Flintstone, only they were dressed a lot nicer, not like cavemen. But they were good bowlers like Fred. I tried to memorize some of their techniques, like I could pick up in a half hour what they had spent years perfecting. They didn't do little ballet steps on their tippy toes like Fred does, but they were sheer poetry in motion. I watched their steps and their swings – beautiful.

I hoped they weren't making fun of me. I was totally out of their league.

It was my turn again (when you are feeling really stupid and would rather be home alphabetizing your spices, your turn comes up more often) and I wasn't paying attention because I was concentrating on my next door neighbors' moves. My plan was to try to use a couple of their moves on this turn. I didn't even notice that I had picked up a 16-pound ball instead of my manageable little 10-pounder. I didn't even notice that it weighed a ton more than my own ball. I approached the lane with my usual method: step left, begin swing, step right, sling bowling ball that is way too heavy for me completely off my fingers and into the Fred Flintstone league. Not only were they fabulous bowlers, they were also extremely adroit at jumping backward from a sitting position. I never saw 4 large men move in a flash – and as a single unit. One of them even screamed with a full soprano voice. I don't think I hit anybody.

That was the end of my bowling session. I offered to keep score for the rest of the group. I did manage to remember how to keep score from my college days, not that there were any good scores to mark down after my little demonstration. My teammates kept giggling and were totally useless with a bowling ball.

I made a promise to the manager of that bowling establishment to never darken his doors again. The Fred Flintstone league must have been very special to him. Now I am back to Moron status on the bowling circuit, which is fine with me, but my spices are all in order from Allspice to Turmeric.

THE TRAVELING CHRISTMAS TREE

Dear Jennifer,

It is probably too late to tell you this, but if you have any overseas packages to be delivered for Christmas, they should have been mailed in October.

A few years ago, a friend of mine was serving as a missionary in Hong Kong. Our Sunday school class wanted to send her a care package for Christmas so she would have some presents to open and not feel so lonely away from friends and family. We packed a good-sized box full of treats, small gift wrapped packages, a few good snacks, and a tiny Christmas tree with some unbreakable ornaments. I observed the deadline of October 15 for getting it to the post office. That morning I walked into the post office and plopped my package down on the counter. The young man behind the counter looked at my package and said, "Hmm. Hong Kong. That's in Japan, isn't it?"

Me: No. China.
Him: Are you sure?
Me: I promise.
Him (rubbing his chin): Well, I wonder when that happened.
Me: Uh … actually, it has been a part of China for a really long time.
Him: Are you sure?
Me: Trust me. (I pushed my glasses down my nose and looked over the rims at him. It gives me the appearance of having superior intellect at times like this).
Him: Okay, if you say so. I know Korea is around there somewhere, too.
Me: You are quite erudite in geography.
Him: I'm what?
Me: Never mind.

He didn't buy the superior intellect look. In retrospect, I should've picked up my package and taken it to a different post office. But I thought I explained well enough where Hong Kong is (and has been for a long time now) and I was already late for work after our geography lesson.

I sent my friend an email that afternoon and told her to expect a Christmas package in December. I don't know where that little package went, but it must have taken the full Asian tour. My friend received her package in February. She pulled out the little Christmas tree, put cute hearts all over it, and celebrated Valentine's Day.

CHRISTMAS SHOPPING

Dear Jennifer,

I will apologize in advance for anything I mess up at the office over the next few days. I can only blame it on the month of December. You know how crazy it gets – setting up the new line for next season – Thanksgiving arriving late this year - half the department using up vacation days – online shopping – my undecorated tree – the awful pushing and shoving at the book store – I hope I didn't hurt anybody.

I actually set off the security alarm at the book store. I was getting luckier than I expected so I had to find a basket to carry all my unpaid-for treasures. The baskets are located dangerously close to the entrance. I picked up a basket with my free hand and suddenly sirens were going off all over the place. I didn't feel so bad when the lady behind me did the same thing. Maybe that should be a sign to the person in charge to ease those things further away from the sensors. I already suffer guilt feelings for being so unorganized at work and at home. I sure don't need to add 'shoplifting suspect' to the guilt train.

Things have been so busy I haven't even been able to wrap any presents. My dining room was beginning to look like a distribution center until Hubby felt sorry for me and paid our neighbor Eloise to wrap everything. I have always suffered a long standing Christmas tradition of waiting until the last minute to do a marathon gift wrapping frenzy on Christmas Eve. This is followed the next day by a sleep-deprived headache and a vow to be more prepared next year. The other part of that tradition is that I never carry through with the vow to be more prepared.

I never used to wrap the girls' gifts. I kept them hidden all over the house (with a special decoder book to remind me where everything was stored) and set them out on Christmas Eve after the girls had gone to bed. Every Christmas morning I wondered why they weren't thrilled, overjoyed, any enthusiastic emotion will do here. Weeping with gratitude maybe. I got nothing. Then I discovered that they were sneaking downstairs in the middle of the night to do a thorough survey of all their loot. Well, that just bugged me. I wanted to see that 'oh, it's just what I always wanted' look. Instead I got 'what's for breakfast, Ma?'

After the girls' cruel behavior was exposed, I got my revenge. The next year, all gifts were wrapped and in code. No to-from tags. Only I knew which gift wrap was assigned to which girl. It. Drove. Them. Nuts.

The girls are all grown up now with families of their own, so I have a lot more gifts to wrap. And a new wave of gifts was delivered this week. I'm trying to get on Eloise's gift wrapping schedule so she can finish up.

I've noticed that now when my online orders arrive, I get a picture of my front porch with packages sitting on it. Someone around here seriously needs to sweep that porch.

Dear Santa, if you will clean my front porch on Christmas Eve, I promise to try to sweep it, maybe in June and again in October. Also, if you will inspire my grandchildren to sneak and take a peek at their gifts to irritate their moms, I will thank you with any enthusiastic emotion you deem acceptable.

LIFE IN COVID CAPTIVITY, WEEK 1

Dear Jennifer,

How is your week going? This is how my first week of working remotely from home went:

Monday
Our team worked as hard as we could, preparing to start working from home on Tuesday. We took time for lunch at our favorite restaurant, which we do every Monday. Our Monday lunches have become a tradition for us. The Monday special is a burrito with free drink. That's sweet tea with of pile of lemon wedges for me. We called it our Last Lunch. It was a little sad. The laptop I ordered never arrived, since it was probably on the same truck with two tons of toilet paper, so I borrowed an old used one. My beloved coworkers and I packed up all the equipment we would need for a two-week stay at home and gave a final fist-bump goodbye. Not as personal as a hug, but it was as close as we were willing to get.

At home Hubby spent four hours helping me set up my little office. Thank goodness, we are empty nesters and I had a free bedroom to use as my office. He got me two large monitors from his stash (thank goodness, Hubby is a computer geek) and all the necessary cables that go with them. These monitors are so large my neighbor can probably read them from across the street. But the nice thing is – I won't have to squint to read the tiny print on the old borrowed laptop. Connecting, testing, reconnecting, and retesting took a lot of time. And my laptop didn't recognize my home printer. Hubby worked on that for a long, long time before telling me it was a Help Desk issue. He was finally satisfied that everything but the printer was working and I was ready to start my first workday from home.

Tuesday
I got up early and went to the grocery store for toilet paper. None. And not much of anything else either, unless I was in

need of caviar or gorgonzola cheese. I went home and started working in my new office with a view. Quite nice. Then I needed to print. So I called the Help Desk. They might possibly be the most overwhelmed group in the world this week. My call didn't even go to voice mail. I didn't even get that 'your call is very important to us' message. Just silence. It was clearly time to think outside the box. So I came up with a brilliant scheme: I emailed my print to my personal email, pulled my personal email up on a home computer with its own separate keyboard, mouse and monitor, and sent my print to our home printer - bingo. Very clever, but I was sure hoping that I didn't have to go through that rigmarole every time I needed to print.

Wednesday

Armed with a laptop, home computer, two keyboards, two mice and two monitors, I was ready to roll. Things were going swell. I got a lot of work done and printed everything I needed to print. I decided to go grocery shopping at lunch. I went to a new grocery store. No TP. From there I went to a discount store. No TP. A different grocery store. No TP. Drugstore. No TP. You can make a lot of stops during your lunch hour if you don't really do anything at each location. We have a whole unopened package of TP at home. I just want to prove to myself that I can find a package somewhere. Remember what Darth Vader said to Luke? "It is your destiny." On the bright side, I have learned the locations of several promising grocery stores.

Thursday

I gave the original grocery store another chance on TP. Nope. Cutting up an old T-shirt into large squares is beginning to appeal to me. I got an email from someone I never heard of, telling me that my request for a laptop had been rejected. I haven't been rejected since twelfth grade when Barton Jeffries stood me up for the bus drivers' Christmas party. I didn't really want to go. I wasn't even a bus driver. But it would have been less embarrassing if I could have made that decision by myself. The laptop is like TP. I don't really need it, but when they are keeping it from me, I want it more than anything.

Friday

Thankfully, Friday was rather slow. Then we got the email from upper management, extending our exile another week. I can hang on if Hubby can. We stopped at three stores on the way to the cabin. No TP. I made plans to start gathering my old T-shirts.

LIFE IN COVID CAPTIVITY, WEEK 2

Dear Jennifer,

Monday
I sat at my large desk and gazed out my large window, enjoying the view of workmen digging up my neighbor's front yard. Not that digging up someone's front yard was all that entertaining, I was just glad it wasn't MY front yard. I worked steadily all day, and loved coming to work in my stretchy pants. I'm thinking of going to HR with some new dress code ideas when all the dust settles. Then the old borrowed laptop began to have a seizure.

Tuesday
The laptop was even sicker than it was on Monday. It started ending my sessions before I told it to end them, then it started blue screening. Hubby referred to this as BSOD (blue screen of death). I thought he was spelling a new bad word, because he doesn't use bad words. I don't either, but I am considering taking up the habit. I rebooted and everything seemed fine for a little while. After another hour of begging the old borrowed laptop to please work, it went into a sudden crash dump and began making a groaning, grinding sound. End of laptop. In my frustration, I may have accidentally pounded it with a hammer eight or nine times to try to fix it. Hubby and I spent the next couple of hours disconnecting the old, borrowed, lifeless laptop and reconnecting, downloading, and some other hardware terms I can't understand on an old reliable laptop we have lying around. Thank goodness for the computer geek at my house.

Wednesday
I arrived at my large office with view and got everything up and running, after signing in and entering verification codes about twelve times. Then the Internet went down. Our internet provider hates my neighborhood almost as much as I hate our internet provider. I missed a fabric conference call. Oh, well - there's a bright side to everything. The internet came back up

and I got to go through the whole process of signing in and getting verification codes again. We listened to the governor's Stay at Home message and afterward I saw an email about India being on lockdown for 21 days. I took two chocolate truffles to calm my nerves.

Thursday
Every electronic gadget in my office was actually working. I had a lunchtime appointment for grocery pickup. Guess what item they could not fill from my order? Their paper products screen should not have offered this as available when I was selecting my items. When I got home I started trying to order next week's groceries to do my part for social distancing. After checking the nine closest stores to me and finding all their time slots filled, I gave up. Store #10 was 45 miles away, so it seemed smarter just to do my own shopping and not breathe while I'm in the store.

Friday
Vacation day! I worked harder at the cabin than I ever have at the office. But the exercise was good for me. I've been going a little soft sitting there every day in my stretchy pants. Bea sent me a reminder the other day to be sure and try my jeans on every few days because pajamas will have you believe all is well with the world. The toilet paper jokes have been going around. Some of them are very humorous, but I would enjoy them more if I could load a few rolls in the back of my car.

COVID TP CHASE

Dear Jennifer,

My latest adventure was in the bathroom tissue and paper towel aisle at the big box store. It was a very short adventure because there was no paper. Not a single package. Not even facial tissues. I blame this on the media. They've gotten hoarders worked up to a fever pitch.

I am a very organized person. I keep a magnetic note pad on the fridge and when we are running low on a grocery item, it is written down on the list. In 47 years of being a grown-up (meaning that I have been buying my own groceries since I was young – very, very young), I've never run out of food or household supplies. Hence, my irritation in the big box store when I went for my single package of bathroom tissue and couldn't get any. This was worse than any milk and bread rush just before a big snow; big around here being greater than two inches. I hope you aren't a hoarder, because I am about to get insulting.

Liquid soap. Why are all the liquid soap shelves empty? This disturbs me. I get the TP rush. Here in the South when the meteorologist says the words ice, sleet or snow, we all make a mad dash to the store for TP, bread and milk. And at my house we add cheese, crackers, chips and chocolate – all the important C foods. But liquid soap? Why is there a sudden need for my fellow citizens to wash their hands? This borders on gross. Aren't these people in the habit of washing their hands on a regular basis by now? When the virus scare is over, are they going back to *not* washing their hands? I may never touch anything in public again.

Anyway, as I stood there staring at the completely empty paper products aisle, wondering if perhaps a little old lady had just walked out with the last package of Quilted Northern and I might still have time to jump her from behind in the parking lot, a very nice customer told me about the RV toilet paper in the camping section. Well, no, not by the time I got over there. So I went to a regular grocery store. No paper. Then I went to a really cheap store that has no business being in business. None. Then the drug store. Nada. I just looked for the empty shelves. Finding the correct aisle was faster that way. And then I was out of store options because our little mountain town is, well, little.

Not only am I very organized, I am also a professional planner, as you well know. A good planner always has a Plan B. My Plan B is the stack of fast food drive through napkins in the glove compartment of Hubby's truck. Plan C is something I discovered on the internet, probably written by a survivalist. Mullein is a wild plant that grows everywhere, including my property, and is known by various names, such as 'velvet leaf'. Doesn't that sound comfy? It is also called 'cowboy toilet paper'. I figure if it's good enough for a cowboy, it's good enough for me. I can always fall back on those old T-shirts, if all else fails. I would really hate to mistreat an old T-shirt like that.

COVID TP SUCCESS

Dear Jennifer,

I have 88 rolls of toilet paper. Most of them are of newspaper quality, nevertheless, I have reached my goal. I have made it to the top. But that heady rush I was expecting to feel just isn't there. Where is that sense of satisfaction? Now I am experiencing that same feeling you get after all the Christmas presents have been opened: total letdown. There is only one cure for reaching all your goals: set new goals. At this point, I am considering my next quest. Flour? Sugar? Cans of tuna? Would you believe the grocery store's marshmallow supply was depleted last week? What sort of global emergency requires hoarding marshmallows?

In other news . . .
With Bea working at home a few days per week, she has started Belle on potty training classes. What a brilliant child. Belle performs best if there is a camera nearby. Definitely not an introvert. While other grandmothers are showing off pictures of their grandkids winning soccer trophies, I'm showing off Belle sitting in her winning position. There must be a strong potty/toilet paper chemical in my DNA.

Last weekend Hubby and I began our yearly mission to eradicate kudzu from the globe. Okay, it's perfectly acceptable in Japan, which I don't get, but it's a pandemic in the southeastern US. I was digging away at a big crown root, aware that I was parked directly over a briar. When it finally became too uncomfortable, I stood up and realized I was sitting on that old barbed wire fencing we accidentally found last year. Now I am searching through my medical records to find when I had my last tetanus shot. Wouldn't it be embarrassing to get tetanus with all the coronavirus germs floating around?

Speaking of the coronavirus, I made my own designer mask so that I can safely go out in public more fashionably. Okay, I am wearing stretchy pants all day, but I need my masks to make a statement. I followed the sewing instructions exactly and wound up wearing a mask that perfectly fits my chin, but cups my lower eyelids. Most uncomfortable, and makes wearing glasses impossible. Also, the elastic strap around my ears is so tight, it pulls my ears forward, making me look like a close relative of Dopey. I guess the pattern makers were in too much of a hurry to check the specs on this pattern. Time for alterations or better yet, time to buy a couple of comfortable masks designed and sewn by professionals.

COVID MASK ANXIETY

Dear Jennifer,

I worked and worked on that mask but I couldn't make it comfortable or attractive. It just looked ridiculous. Unfortunately, the store-bought masks haven't arrived yet. Since it was the right thing to do, and the Covid police will arrest you if you aren't suffering behind a mask of some sort, I put it on when we arrived at a grocery store in a little town late Sunday. It was on the way home and nobody knew me there, so I figured it couldn't hurt.

I put that baby on and immediately, my glasses started steaming up. Nobody said anything about obscured vision as a side effect. So I felt my way around the produce section, careful to not touch anything unless I was prepared to buy. I tried not to breathe in order to keep the steam content down, but that just wasn't going to happen. It's too bad I didn't have a Seeing Eye dog in there with me. In addition, the elastic bands were still too short, so there I was fumbling my way from aisle to aisle with foggy glasses and Dopey ears. The management people are probably still enjoying the show on their security cameras.

Not knowing my way around the little store, I had to retrace my steps several times. I probably made figure 8's all over the place. I picked up a few things in every department, except the paper aisle, of course. I knew that once I had 88 rolls of my own, the shelves would be full to overflowing. In addition to having no idea where anything was, I heard the announcement that the store would be closing early for Easter in just a few short minutes. Now my anxiety level was raised. I grabbed cookies, 2 pounds of ground beef, hamburger buns, bananas, sandwich bread - you know - the basics.

I found the front of the store and for some stupid reason went to the self-check aisle. Never having been there, with the store closing in a few short minutes, it would have been much smarter to let a professional check me out. But that mask was intimidating me and making my decisions for me. And there was an old hippie guy behind me, so for another stupid reason, I thought I needed to hurry and get the job done and get out of his way. He seemed pretty cool (old hippie guys are almost always pretty cool), so there really was no reason for me to over-stress on this. That horrid mask was making me stress over everything.

I must have looked pretty pathetic because the little girl that mans the self-check area came over to help me.

Cashier: Have you ever shopped with us before?
Me (with mask on): No an I cat fee anyfing wif dif mafk on.
Cashier: Well, I'll be happy to help you.
Me (with mask on): Fank you very mutt for your hep.

We finally got the job done. I grabbed my three bags and exited the store as they were locking late arrivals out. I got in the truck and told Hubby about all the goodies I had stocked up on. Could he have gone in there with me for moral support? No, he was on the phone with our friend helping him with a WiFi issue. Frankly, dealing with fogged up glasses, Dopey ears, and an old hippie guy was preferable to dealing with our friend over a WiFi issue.

We got home a half hour later and I unpacked all my treasures. As I was putting away the perishables, I began getting that little nagging feeling you get when you know things just aren't quite right. So I pulled out my receipt and realized that my 2 pounds of ground beef were still sitting at the self-check counter. Or, more likely, the old hippie guy just won $11.11 worth of free hamburger. I hope he enjoys it. Hubby and I have been enjoying banana sandwich buns.

SOCIAL DISTANCING FAUX PAS

Dear Jennifer,

When we left for the cabin on Friday we stopped at an old grocery store outside of town that has been operating since Hubby was a little boy. I guess they have added electricity since then. Their reputation for good meats drew us there. And waiting in line to get in was a really big thrill. They let five shoppers in at a time and I had to wait quite a while for my turn. I haven't waited that long for food since that fancy restaurant opened up downtown a few years ago. The two ladies in front of me outside the store kept turning around and staring at me. I figured they were making fun of my mask. Or coveting it. Those things can go either way. But then I realized I was standing less than six feet away from them. I was probably as close as four feet. What was I thinking? I'm so glad I took those two steps back before the social distancing police gave me a citation.

Once inside the store I picked up a large package of ground beef and a few 'non-meat' items. I had waited in line for so long, I had to make the trip worth my while. There was plenty of cheap toilet paper for sale, no limit, which was understandable. We have tons of sandpaper in the garage so I left their cheap TP on the shelf.

We stopped at another store closer to the cabin so we could pick up some ice cream and a pizza, something we couldn't grab earlier because ice cream just doesn't hang in there for the long haul, no matter how good the cooler is. Pizza must be on the list of things to hoard in that little town. My brand of pizza was left behind and I snatched it up before another shopper spotted it. In my experience, even if a shopper hasn't planned on a particular purchase, if she sees a half empty shelf, her rational thinking goes out the door and she knocks other shoppers out of her way to get what's left. At least that's how it is when *I* see a half empty shelf.

I rounded another couple of aisles and then I saw it: the toilet paper shelf had five packages of Quilted Northern (3-ply). I heard angels singing. I saw rainbows and butterflies. It didn't matter that I still have 84 rolls of TP at home. I tenderly picked up a 12-double-rolls-equals-18-rolls package and hugged it affectionately, whispering softly, "I have missed you so much". I left the remaining four packages on the shelf because I'm not a TP weirdo.

We arrived at the cabin late in the afternoon and spotted large tufts of insulation on the grass. Hmm...

We unpacked and got comfortable and cozy inside. It was just cool enough to have a fire in the fireplace. It was so quiet and peaceful up there. No traffic noises. No sirens. Just scratching in the corner of the bedroom ceiling. Scratching? Then the tufts of insulation came to mind. We started calling pest control people. Would you believe most pest control companies won't come for a visit once you tell them your dwelling has a metal roof? We finally found a nice young man who was willing to fix the damages for a small fortune. As it turned out, a bird was the critter responsible for making such a mess.

Now I'm wondering - should I stuff that bird and mount it on the roof to serve as a warning to the others? Or will it start bringing its friends over to intimidate us? I hope it never heard of Alfred Hitchcock.

SOCIAL DISTANCING CORRECTNESS

Dear Jennifer,

I heard that there are several cases of the virus at the big chicken processing plant, so I started thinking. I missed out on the TP, paper towel and ground beef frenzy. I plan to be involved in any potential chicken frenzies. Obviously, there is going to be one, because the chicken processing plant will have to do something serious, like send all the chicken employees home so they can disinfect. And without chicken in my house, we might have to learn to like tofu. Gag me with a spoon.

I went to the grocery store and bought a fair amount of chicken. My original plan was to hoard a couple tons of chicken like everyone else, but the classier part of me won out. Also, I don't have a large freezer to store a lot of chicken. Now, toilet paper - you can store that anywhere. Not chicken.

And would you believe this same grocery store's paper aisle is still empty?

Ellen brought the kiddos over for lunch today. We visit with them on Zoom, but it was so nice to see them in 3-D after seven long weeks of separation. Hubby grilled hamburgers and hot dogs in advance and left them on the grill. I set out what they would need: plates, condiments, drinks, etc. Then Hubby and I locked ourselves into our small screened porch and watched them play and eat their lunch from greater than six feet away.

Sometimes they would stand around and talk to us from a socially acceptable distance. We felt like a zoo exhibit. Athena, Hawkins and Julius can tell all their friends they saw male and female old people in their natural habitat: a back porch.

COVID REFLECTIONS

Dear Jennifer,

Reflecting on the last few weeks in quarantine, I have made a few profound observations:

• There are 999,999 combinations of security codes for getting logged in to our systems at home
• Most of them have been texted to my phone
• When I'm sitting in my large beautiful office with a view and if I have my high-powered binoculars handy, I can see the secret ingredient my neighbor adds to her fabulous spaghetti sauce. Sorry I can't share that information with you. Now it's *my* secret ingredient.
• I have worked near my husband for over nine weeks and hardly considered calling a divorce attorney
• Or the homicide squad
• You can beat a laptop to death with a hammer and it will still work, and just as slowly as before
• I have forgotten how to apply mascara
• I have saved $750 by not eating out
• I have spent $1,000 more on groceries by eating in
• I learned a few new recipes
• Some of them were good
• Canned biscuits aren't awful if you disguise them with lots and lots of herbs and spices
• If I were meant to wear a mask, I would've been born looking like a raccoon
• When we go back to the office our company should seriously consider relaxing our dress code to allow pajama pants
• And maybe fuzzy bunny slippers

A LOT OF HOT AIR

Dear Jennifer,

Last Friday began a week's vacation, so on the way to the cabin we stopped at the store for some new inner tubes. Ellen and Hubby had discussed a possible tubing activity when Ellen's family comes up Sunday for Father's Day. We grabbed the only 4 inner tubes they had.

On Saturday, Hubby wanted to hit another store in town to check out their inner tube supply and we picked up 4 more. Then he saw a tube that holds a cooler or 2 small boys. So that went into the cart. I finally convinced Hubby that we had a sufficient number of tubes to do the job and pointed the cart toward the register.

Then we went home with plans to start inflating a truck full of inner tubes. We went down to the barn and set up a blow up area. Hubby got 2 tubes inflated. On tube #3, the air compressor died. He tried fixing it. We googled dead air compressors. We were running out of time. Father's Day was approaching. We knew we had to go back to town and get another compressor (30-minute drive each way, by the way). To save money, Hubby offered to start blowing them up the old fashioned way. Seriously? We bought 9, you've finished 2, there are 3 more old tubes in the cabin waiting to be inflated, and you only have 2 lungs. There's a mathematical formula in there somewhere and you simply aren't adding up.

We went to the farm supply store (big guy toy store) and bought Hubby's dream compressor: an upright 30-gallon baby on wheels. Piece of cake. Well, making the purchase was a piece of cake. And by the way, since a new air compressor wasn't on the budget for this year, it had to come out of the Christmas budget. I hope the girls understand that the air compressor they're getting for Christmas has to remain in our barn.

Problem: how do you lift a 400-pound air compressor onto the bed of a truck? Easy. Let the store employees use their fork lift.

Next problem: how do you stabilize a 400-pound air compressor after the store employees leave it standing on top of a pallet in the truck bed and run back into the store? Easy. Simply work the compressor off the pallet, slowly and carefully, then you 'walk' the compressor over to the corner between the tailgate and the wheel well, then you take the pallet and use it as a wedge to prevent the compressor from moving from side to side, then you take a good length of quality rope, which Hubby always carries in the truck, and you loop rope around, through, over and under eye bolts and compressor handles until it won't move at all.

Next problem: how do you keep a 400-pound air compressor from wobbling once the truck is in motion? Easy. Simply drive 20 mph and no faster. There sure was a lot of horn beeping on the road that night. And there must've been some sort of parade in town. There were a lot of vehicles behind us.

Next problem: after you get home how do you get a 400-pound air compressor off the bed of the truck without that handy fork lift back in town? Easy. Simply untie the compressor and roll it to the tailgate, create a pulley system with that quality rope that Hubby keeps in his truck, and ease the compressor down a ramp. Fortunately, Hubby was a Boy Scout, always prepared and in this case had 2 ramps in the barn. While Hubby was working through this problem, I sneaked away for a sandwich. It was 8:00 at night and I'm not at my best when I'm starving to death.

We were ready to start our mass assembly and churn out some river rafting gear! Hubby plugged up the compressor, hit the ON switch, and let 'er rip. Blew a fuse. The barn was in total darkness.

River rafting was getting just a little annoying by this time. Hubby ran 3 drop cords end-to-end from the shed at the top of the hill to supply the power. Didn't work. He finally drew on his engineering DNA and came up with a fix which I can't even begin to describe because I don't have any engineering genes. We finally got all the tubes ready for the water. I can't give you an exact total of tubes anymore because the numbers keep running together. It was enough to know there were more available tubes than people needing them.

Ellen's family arrived on Sunday around lunchtime to celebrate Father's Day – just about a half hour before the thunder, lightning and pouring rain began.

ANOTHER BAT TALE

Dear Jennifer,

More bat drama …

I was grown up and married, and working at the office when Hubby called me one day from home. He had just gotten home from school (he was a public school teacher at the time, which is totally irrelevant to this story), and as he was telling me about his exciting day teaching algebra, a bat flew past him. Inside our house.

Naturally, I had flashbacks of Granny's old farmhouse, so I told him to call me back when the matter was resolved. Then I hung up on him. I didn't think that was rude. He had a job to do and I was keeping him from doing it as long as I was on the phone. This is what ensued:

By the time Hubby hung up the phone (after being hung up on), the bat was nowhere in sight. Hubby was still wearing his nice teacher clothes and figured this would be a dirty job, so his first thought was to change into bat man clothes, then seek out and eradicate. He gathered his 'changing the oil' ensemble - old torn jeans and stained sweatshirt - and laid them on the bed. Then he took off his nice teacher outfit. Be patient with me here, it all comes together in a minute.

He was down to his boxers when – you guessed it – he spotted the bat. It was perched on a lamp shade. I was so glad I didn't see that. The lamp was on my side of the bed. But Hubby knew if he took the time to get dressed he would probably lose sight of the bat again. So he grabbed a blanket and threw it over the bat, lamp, shade, and whatever else was in the way.

Hubby took the whole thing out to the deck to free the bat and be done with this distasteful job. And speaking of distasteful, he turned to go back inside and saw our next door neighbor on her deck. She waved, said "hello" and giggled. She was gracious enough not to say, "Nice shorts", but she also didn't go back inside. She just stood there smiling at him. She didn't even have the decency to blush. Really, she should have been a little ashamed of herself.

Hubby was mortified. First, he had to rid our house of an old bat, and then he had to endure a fair amount of torture from the old bat next door. She had never been very friendly, but after that day, she was always smiling and waving to Hubby from her yard. She never smiled or waved to me. She only saved the smiles and waves for Hubby. I suppose if I had wanted her to be nice to me I should've worn boxers outside.

LAWN MOWER REPAIR

Dear Jennifer,

When we inherited our mountain property 20 years ago, there was a lot of work to be done. We were basically starting from scratch. Our agreement was, and still is, to divide the work 50-50. It has been a fair deal so far. I have helped dredge ditches and do landscaping with Hubby, and he has helped me inside with vacuuming (I have this bad back, you know) and general cleaning. He even cooks occasionally. His campfire burgers are legendary. He also helps me in the eradication of kudzu, which you should know by now, is my own personal crusade.

Last Saturday at the cabin Hubby was mowing the yard and something broke under the lawn mower. The motor seemed fine; it just didn't want to mow any more. Repair time. There were only the two of us and Hubby needed an assistant. Guess who? Fortunately, we have a nice barn to work in, so things could have been worse. Actually, things did get worse, but that's for later.

The first step was to read the directions. That's always my job because I'm the wife. Wives read directions. The second step was to *understand* the directions. After several minutes of head scratching, we began to understand that their 'retainer spring' was our 'cotter pin'. I knew then that if just translating the 'how-to' section was this difficult, it was going to be a long day. After we removed the mowing deck from the mower - and I do mean WE - Hubby discovered that a part had broken its welded connections in several places. Now we were faced with 3 options: spend way too much money on a new mower, find a welder in the mountains after lunch on Saturday, or try bolting it back on.

First of all, we don't have lawn mower money in the budget, although I could borrow a little from my mascara and gasoline funds, which I am not using right now, thanks to working remotely. Second, getting a mountain welder to your house

96

NOW means that you live in a fenced in game preserve and it's huntin' season. The reason for the extreme longevity in mountain people is that they don't stress and get in a hurry. No, you make an appointment for next week and they will get around to it sometime. The last time I called someone to get the flying squirrels out of the attic, he said he would be over 'this evenin'. ('This evenin' in the mountains is mid to late afternoon. Today.) He didn't come that afternoon, that evening, or that week. He also didn't return my calls. He'll never call now after he reads the review I left on the internet. Anyway, we knew inviting a welder to our cabin for an emergency visit would be a waste of time. So, we went with Option 3 - bolting it back on. Definitely a DIY project.

In case you don't drill much, I will share the difficulties of drilling through a metal mowing deck. For one thing, it's cozy down there and the manufacturer didn't leave any extra room for bolts. That's why they welded it in the first place. For another thing, there are a lot of moving parts down there, so you have to be careful that those moving parts don't bump into bolts that were never meant to hang out there. You also need some bolts. Hubby just happened to have some. I'm so lucky that he is always prepared. If he wasn't so organized I would have been forced to spend the day reading a cozy mystery. Finally, when the tip of your drill bit breaks off, you have to get creative. You have to drill the hole with a smaller bit, and then finish it out with the damaged one. I really hope I don't have to retain all this knowledge for a future project.

This sounds pretty streamlined, doesn't it? That bolting part took 3 hours. But then it was time for the big challenge: putting the mower deck belt back on. When the mower broke, it sort of chewed up the old belt. The belt with some give. Hubby just happened to have a replacement. A replacement belt that had never been stretched even a little bit. According to the directions, we had to put the mower deck back into place and THEN after the deck was completely under the mower, fit the belt onto the pulleys. I was getting tired and just a tad bit grumpy. Fortunately, we had that nice barn with a concrete floor - and - a piece of outdoor carpet. So I got to lie on the concrete floor in luxurious comfort as I fought to get the belt around that last pulley - the pulley hardest to reach. In the meantime, Hubby was reaching under there and pushing another pulley toward me to give me some slack. It wasn't enough.

We traded places. I got to push the pulley to give HIM extra slack. Still didn't work. As an aside, I think 'pushing pulleys' sounds funny. Since I am sort of a simpleton about machinery and repairs, I asked a really stupid question. Couldn't we ignore the directions just this once and fit the belt around the most inaccessible pulley first, and then choose a more convenient pulley to force the belt on at the end of the process? Okay, sometimes I am a genius. The belt went on. I tried to act humble. Hubby took the mower out for a test mow and came back for an inspection.

He didn't like what he saw underneath. I liked it just fine. Okay, I didn't look, but I just knew it looked great. Besides, it was supper time. One of the pulleys was too close to a big spring and Hubby just wasn't satisfied with its potential for disaster. He is a trouble shooter from way back and likes to get things right with no surprises later. So we had to pull the deck back out. Sadly, I knew just what to do, and I was seriously questioning this whole 50-50 working arrangement we had agreed to. Maybe we could renegotiate and work out a 75-25 deal if I find my own kudzu. Hubby added one more bolt. I was seriously hoping this would work, because there didn't seem to be any more free space for another bolt. Then we put the deck back in place, including the stubborn belt. That piece of carpet was looking so good by this time, I just wanted to crawl right under the mower and take a nap there. Hubby took it out for another test mow and came back for another inspection. I held my breath. I was too tired to hold anything else.

Hubby was satisfied with what he saw. And it only took 6 hours of heavy labor. How do women with manicures and nice hair get anything done? I learned three valuable things while engaged in this activity:

1. I can remove and reattach a mowing deck in my sleep.
2. Mountain men are pretty smart to avoid jobs on Saturday afternoons.
3. Now I can recognize a broken mower deck sound so next time I hear it, I can run and hide in a big patch of kudzu.

I KILL MY FIRST DEERE

Dear Jennifer,

While we are on a lawn mower theme, I will confess to you that I am no better at mowing a yard than I am at playing field hockey. One day Hubby had a lot to do away from home and it was yard mowing day. He asked Bea and me very nicely if we would mow for him. This was just about the last thing I wanted to do but he would do most anything for me if I asked, so I agreed. Bea didn't mind at all. She thought it was like driving. Obviously, she didn't have her license yet.

We have an acre lot so eventually the John Deere was thirsty. Bea coasted up to the shed and told me she needed a fill-up. I knew how to pour gas so I did that rather well. Then Bea checked the oil and told me it was down and we should add a quart so I did that as well.

You might not know this, but a small John Deere lawn mower holds 1.5 quarts of oil. When the mower is running the oil is dispersed throughout the engine lubricating all the necessary parts. It isn't just resting in a little bowl down there somewhere. It sounds like I know what I'm talking about, right? That's because I do. Now. I learned all this from the lecture I got when Hubby came home and found out that I had drowned his beloved John Deere with a whole extra quart of oil.

In my defense, Bea is to blame. She told me to do it. I know that sounds like an excuse little kids use, but Bea was always smarter than I so if she told me to do something mechanical I did it. But she was young and cute and I was in charge, so it was my fault.

In addition to the lecture about oil, Hubby also informed me that John Deere was probably going to die. I had killed it. I didn't believe that for a minute. Surely he was exaggerating. To prove it to me Hubby started up the mower and we heard a loud 'BOOM'. It was followed by a huge plume of blue-grey smoke pouring out the back. Every man in the neighborhood came running over. I'm pretty sure the local news team was there filming for the 6:00 lead story. I stayed inside and peeked out from behind the drapes. They all knew what had happened and they all knew who did it. And not a single man blamed Bea.

Hubby had to go to the lawn mower store and buy a new mower. It wasn't a John Deere – he couldn't afford another one. He arranged to have the new mower delivered to our house and the dead Deere picked up. When the store employee brought it over, I had to be the one to inform him that he was taking the John Deere back with him. He asked if they were supposed to repair it, then return it to our house and I explained what I had done. "Oh," was all he said. But he said it with a very sad face. I guess he already knew what happens when you overfeed a mower. Bea and I must've been the only 2 people in town who didn't have this valuable information stored somewhere.

It was several years before Hubby let me near a mower again. It was another one of those times when he was exceedingly busy. It was a pretty day and I didn't mind (too much) so I had the entire front yard mowed when he returned. I didn't think Hubby was that picky. He didn't like the corduroy effect I had given our yard. Did you know when you mow the yard you should drive so that the front wheels roll *beside* the mashed down grass from the impression of the wheels from the previous cycle? I do now. I was placing the front wheel right *on* the mashed grass. After it relaxed it popped right back up. Our whole front yard had a sort of ribbed effect. It looked like Mr. T had designed our yard himself. Hubby jumped right on the mower and re-mowed the yard before any of the guy neighbors could see it and think Hubby had redesigned the Fescue.

The lady next door came by and asked why Hubby didn't like the Mohawk hairdo I gave the yard. I guess if ladies were noticing the grass it must've been really bad. On the bright side, these days when Hubby is mowing the yard he tells me to go inside where it's safe. I know that he means the grass and the mower will be safe, but that's okay.

KILLER BEES

Dear Jennifer,

Time for a story from the Family Vault of Mostly True Tales...

Several years ago – when we had a camper trailer instead of a cabin – we had just arrived with all our stuff for the first nice weekend of the season and were just as snippy with each other as was possible. I can't remember what we were fussing about. I only remember that it was probably his fault, since it almost always is.

Hubby was on one side of the camper hooking up the water and electricity. I was on the other side letting the step down and preparing to enter with bags of groceries. Suddenly, I was covered with yellow jackets. Or maybe it was killer bees. Yes, I'm sure they were killer bees. They had been very busy in early spring while we were not there, building a nest between the camper's rock guard and the kitchen window. I felt like I was a nameless victim in a cheap horror movie (the uncredited actor with no speaking parts, so you know right from the start who's gonna get killed). I quickly forgot that I wasn't speaking to Hubby and started screaming his name because, as the man of the house, or the camper as it were, it was his job to protect me. He yelled, "Start running!" Hubby is my hero.

You might not be aware of this but when I am in a panic situation, my normal objective thinking mechanism basically shuts down. All I could think of was that if you want to get away from a swarm of bees, you have to get under water. And the river was about a third of a mile run from there, down our steep, long, curved driveway, across a one-lane paved road, down a one-lane dirt road, and into the water – all at about a 200 foot drop in elevation. I had that map in my head as I began running. And I discovered that I can run really fast when I absolutely must. Fortunately, I didn't have to run that far.

103

They must have thought I was running faster than they could fly. When I had only run 20 or 30 feet, they made a sharp left turn and a bee line toward Hubby. Poor guy had his shirt off. Suddenly, he was wearing a bee vest (add another uncredited actor with no speaking parts to this cheap horror movie). We were definitely the victims of a sting operation. I forgave him for every stupid thing he had done that day, whatever that was at the time. And being the positive thinker that I am, I was tickled that I didn't have to run all the way to the river.

Fortunately, Cousin Ambrose heard my shrieks all the way over at his house (down the steep driveway and around 2 curves) and brought over a can of something potent. He has a real ear for 'BEES!' screams. Then he left us so we could start spraying. Hubby took the can and I had the water hose with a spray nozzle. We looked like two good guys in a cheap horror movie who go after the monster. Hubby approached the camper slowly and carefully with the can of something potent and said, "Cover me. I'm going in." So, with the spray attachment on the hose I had to shoot down every bee that approached him from the back, sides and top. Yes, the top. One crazy bee kept dive bombing from several feet up. My aim got better with every shot. I missed Hubby's head after the first few tries. We won't tell him that those first few practice squirts might have hit his head on purpose.

The bees were very stubborn and determined to hang on to their turf. We simply could not convince them that it was our turf FIRST. I had to give them points for teamwork, though. They were awfully mean as a unit. Hubby made several valiant attempts to raise the rock guard so that we could get rid of that nest. It seemed a real shame to tear apart all that work. It must have taken them several months of chewing and spitting to accomplish such an impressive hive.

It only took us about six hours to tear it all down and by the end of the day, there were only a few stragglers left. They had probably been shopping out of town and were coming back home for the night, but couldn't find it. Home was splattered all over the grass. We left the rock guard up for the rest of the summer. We weren't taking any chances. And we spent the summer telling and re-telling our bee story. The number of stings increased every time we had a different audience (the old audiences were tired of hearing about it). By Labor Day my sting count was up to about 75 and Hubby only had around 50. Obviously, his story telling isn't as well developed as mine.

PAPASAN CHAIR

Dear Jennifer,

Bea's birthday is this month. I can't believe my baby is so old – already in her 30s. When she was about to turn 14 she begged and pleaded for a Papasan chair for her birthday. I promised her that on her birthday, she and I would go to the Papasan chair store and she could pick out the one she wanted. I wanted to win the Mother of the Year award that year.

Her birthday was on a Thursday that year, the only night of the week that her dad taught an evening class, which will be handy to know later on. It was pouring rain. I am extremely practical so I knew that it would be better to shop during a non-rainy time and I didn't think another thought about going shopping on a miserable night like this one.

Bea came downstairs after dinner dressed and ready to go shopping.

Bea: Mom, why aren't you ready?
Me: Ready for what?
Bea: Ready to go get my Papasan chair.
Me: But it's raining. Let's go Saturday.
Bea: But today is my birthday.
Me: But today it is raining.
Bea: But you promised.
Me: Meet me at the car in 5.

They don't give that Mother of the Year award to just anybody. So we went to the Papasan chair store in the pouring rain. Fortunately, most other shoppers were wisely spending the evening at home so we had the store basically to ourselves.

Bea had no trouble picking out the chair she wanted. She chose a very attractive forest green cushion to go on it. Then she decided it wouldn't be a good nap chair if she didn't have the footstool and matching forest green cushion to go with.

Potential Mother of the Year put everything in the cart except for the skeletal form of the chair. It was much too large for the cart.

Did you ever see a picture of the Arecibo Telescope in Puerto Rico? It was about 1,000 feet across and built just like that Papasan chair. I was thinking about that telescope as I struggled to the checkout lane with this chair in my arms, over my head, rolling it along the floor – I was trying different ways to transport it. It wasn't that heavy; it was just extremely cumbersome.

I paid for Bea's birthday present and ordered her to remain with our cart outside the store under the awning while I went for the car. I was planning to pull my little Volvo sedan up to the curb so that we could at least avoid walking in the rain since we I had to load the car in the rain. Why did we trade that station wagon?

I really needed Hubby and his truck at this point, but he was unavailable. Have you ever attempted to load a 1,000 foot spherical telescope into the trunk of a sedan? Well, don't. You can't do it. Bea was standing there guarding her prize while I was attempting the logistics of the whole thing and while rain was hitting me from all directions. I needed help. I needed Hubby and his truck. Unfortunately, cell phones weren't part of our family yet. It was entirely up to the candidate for Mother of the Year. I was finally able to fit the largest spherical piece just so in the back seat with the bottom rim resting on the floorboard. And it only took about 37 minutes. And that was it for the back seat. The little footstool – it seemed very little compared to its papa – went into the trunk with the 2 cushions.

We were finished. Everything was inside. And we did it without the benefit of a truck. As I was preparing to get into the driver's seat a man approached me in the parking lot and said, "I didn't think you would ever get that thing loaded into your car!"

Okay, I had several retorts from which to choose:

• You are so lacking in good manners that you watched me for 37 minutes and didn't offer to help?

• You are so lacking in good sense that you admitted to a ˙ lady that you watched her struggling in the rain with a spherical telescope?

• Do you have a death wish?

But I kept those remarks to myself because seeing the look of adoration in Bea's eyes made me want to savor that moment and not blow it by losing my temper.

That Papasan chair more than paid for itself. It moved with Bea to college, then graduate school, and on to her first apartment. It was a much loved and useful piece of furniture. After a long tiring day, it seemed to say, "Come over here, Baby, and let's hug," and it would envelope me in its plush forest green cushions. Every now and then, though, it would look at me and whisper, "I didn't think you would ever get me loaded into your car."

TUBING THE NEW

Dear Jennifer,

It's another true, unvarnished tale from the Family Vault. This is about the exciting tubing trip we took on the New River on a cloudy day last weekend.

Cast:
Me
Hubby
Daughter Ellen
Athena, Ellen's 10-year-old daughter with the vivid imagination
Daughter Bea
Cedric, Bea's 15-year-old son, way cool and doesn't like getting his hair messed up
Belle, Bea's 3-year-old daughter, outfitted with twelve separate flotation devices (we could have tied a string to her and let her float overhead)

Jed, our son-in-law, dropped us off at the river landing and we spent some time (maybe an hour and a half) unloading the truck, putting on water shoes and taking pictures. Jed left us there, wishing us a fun trip. He was planning a fun trip of his own with Jarrod, our other son-in-law, and Hawkins and Julius, our other grandsons, at the ice cream parlor in town (loads more fun than tubing in my opinion). We set out on our tubes and began a leisurely float up the river (the New River flows north), enjoying the peaceful scenery and grateful that the clouds were shading us from the hot sun. Athena saw the dark clouds and did NOT want to be in the river. This was after we were in the river, in the tubes, and away from the ramp where we had put in. Jed must have been halfway through a chocolate ice cream cone by this point.

"I wanna get out I wanna get out I wanna get out!!" Since I have already raised my own two children, I didn't even bother to reason with her about the lack of rationale behind her very sincere request. That was her mama's job. I just drifted along. Ellen assured Athena that the forecast was NOT calling for rain (we really did check before we left). We roped our three tubes together to give Athena a sense of security, meaning if she went down, we all went down together (in a gentle lazy river that was about three feet deep in most places). We tubed leisurely along with the current and after a while Athena began to relax. Maybe because she was sharing her mom's tube at that point. It was riding low in the water with two girls on the same tube, by the way.

I'm not sure what triggered Athena's nerves again, but Ellen assured her that dark clouds don't always mean rain. Plink! Plink! Okay, this time the dark clouds meant rain. But it was just a few sprinkles. At first. Then the rainfall got heavy and the bottom fell out. Athena's panic meter began to rise. Ellen assured Athena that rainfall doesn't always mean thunder. Rumble, rumble, rumble. Okay, this time the rainfall meant thunder. Athena simply wasn't having it. She jumped out of her tube and walked on water to climb up the river bank, which was perpendicular to the river and towered six feet over her head. I still don't know how she did that.

Now we had 4 major problems:
1. We were getting pounded by cold rain;
2. It was thundering all around us;
3. Ellen kept making invalid assurances
4. to a 10-year-old who was planning to walk three miles across a field, up a hill, through a briar patch, over a bridge, and down a one-lane road to get home.

By the way, we were at the mouth of Cranberry Creek, where the water flows out of a refrigerator. If you ever want your teeth to chatter in July, I can take you to a place that will accommodate you. We finally peeled Athena off the river bank and onto Hubby. It was a two-fold blessing. She kept her grandpa warm, and got to sit on his stomach which kept her HIGH and dry. While Athena was dry and comfortable, I was soaked. The half of me that was in the river was dryer than the half of me facing the sky.

Then we encountered turbulence. And by turbulence, I mean a whole lot of rocks near the surface and a whole lot of cold water churning around them. My tube simply wasn't going anywhere I aimed it, and neither was Ellen's, since we were still tied together with an empty tube between us, Athena having abandoned us for higher terrain (grandpa's tummy). The water was too deep to dig my feet in and push us in the right direction (the river is three feet in *most* places, not *all* places), so Cedric rescued us. I don't know what his plans were that day, but I'm guessing they didn't include saving our tubes every ten minutes. Fortunately, his hair still looked good.

We finally maneuvered around the rough parts and under a bridge. We could have parked under the bridge for some shelter from the rain, but there was already too much kayak traffic waiting it out there. I could barely see, since my sunglasses were covered in rain water. It hardly mattered, as I didn't need sunglasses anyway, and my tube insisted on floating backwards on this part of the river. But I learned quickly to react when I heard the phrase "bottoms up!" Unfortunately, my bottom didn't go up far enough and anchored itself on a large rock. In canoe terms I think this is called a 'rockopotamus'. I never knew my bottom could pivot. Our entire flotilla pivoted around my tail bone. If I had known I was going to be the anchor butt for the group, I would have done a little reading on the best procedures. I would still be spinning out there like a turtle on its back if Cedric hadn't rescued me again. But he wasn't finished. And every hair was still in place.

Belle is still young and naive, so she thought she was having fun. And she was riding in the tube designed for a cooler, so she was sitting pretty. And she was eating crackers stored in a water-proof box. Yeah, she was living the dream. Eventually we made it to a small island and were having fun skipping rocks when we saw my sons-in-law driving down the river road to pick us up at our rendezvous point. Sweet rescue. If we could just make it a couple hundred more yards. But first we had to get back in the water.

Hindsight being what it is, what we should have done was put in on the back side of the island where the water flows more gently. Instead we chose the churning side. While most of us were parked in the river ready for takeoff, Bea was trying to ease Belle's tube safely back into the water, and Belle was asking for another cracker. Constantly. Suddenly I was attacked by a whole lot of vinyl and some legs. In the center of that vast assemblage was Bea. She and the tubes she was fighting looked like one of those little animals they make out of balloons. Her animal shape could best be compared to a giraffe trying to pour a cat into its carrier. I still don't know how she did that, but I do know that her float was upside down for the rest of the trip. And the entire time Bea was wrestling with her tube while desperately trying to keep her child safe, Belle was chanting, "Mommy, I want another cracker". She's cute, but clueless.

We needed to start edging toward the left bank. If Cedric hadn't been there to keep getting us out of 'hot water' we would be close to West Virginia by now. But at one point the river got so deep he couldn't touch bottom. That made ME nervous, but I wasn't stupid enough to tell Athena, who, by the way, was still sitting pretty on her grandpa's stomach having a blast. Next time I'M sitting on Hubby's stomach so my butt won't get beaten up so badly. Do they make tubes that big? We made it to our landing spot, stepped onto dry land, and I kissed my son-in-law's pickup truck.

We came away from that adventure with four unsolved mysteries:
1. How Athena climbed a 90-degree wall of dirt without rappelling gear
2. How Bea managed to fold herself and a vinyl tube into a hybrid animal shape
3. How Belle managed to consume an entire pack of DRY crackers the whole length of the trip
4. How Cedric's hair managed to stay perfect all day

Stay tuned next week for the conclusion of this exciting tale.

TUBING THE NEW, PART II

Dear Jennifer,

To continue our exciting river tale...

When we got back to the cabin from our river adventure in the pouring rain and constant rumbling thunder, I was very grateful. So grateful, in fact, that I walked right into the house, dripping all over the floor. I did stop to wring my shorts out over the potted plants on the front porch, thinking they might like the taste of river water for a change.

But I wish I had thought ahead and left some towels waiting for me *outside* under the porch roof. I dripped all the way to a bedroom to fetch a towel and some dry underwear and when I turned to walk out of the room, my wet foot slipped on the hardwood floor and down I went. Believe me; they call it a 'hardwood floor' for a very good reason.

You know how your life passes before your eyes when something like that happens? Well mine didn't because it didn't take that long to hit the floor with my tailbone. I was down in a banana peel second. I'm pretty sure I knocked the cabin off its foundation. The kids thought it was a mild 3.6 earthquake. Now I'm walking funny.

As luck would have it, I had an appointment for my annual physical this week. I have been a patient of Dr. Hart for 35 years. He is my kind of guy: cheap. He still has the same 1960s wallpaper and 1940s medical cabinets in his office. The only difference from 35 years ago is that the wallpaper is peeling now. He sees no reason to update the place. He's old, so why shouldn't his office be?

Dr. Hart's nurse, Drusilla, is way past retirement age and is still working to support herself. She is awfully sweet and gives painless shots. I think she went to nursing school when leeches and bloodletting were all the rage. Drusilla gave me my paper shirt with instructions to leave it open in the back, blah, blah, blah, then she left to give me my privacy.

Now we had a problem. My tail was sore and it hurt to move any bodily part south of my belly button. The examining table was very high. Honestly, when you're 5'2", *every* piece of furniture is very high, with the exception of footstools. Struggling to climb up on top of that table without disturbing the large roll of paper toweling they stretch across there, AND maintain my dignity while keeping that paper shirt on was practically impossible. The paper shirt was 'one size fits most'. Most in this case means 'most of us in the room at the same time'. Three more of me could have fit in that shirt. Sasquatch would have found it too large. Naturally, it kept slipping off one side or the other. I tried standing in front of the table and hopping up onto it backwards. Seriously? Did I hit my head when I fell the other day? I tried easing one cheek at a time up there, but my cheeks were two feet below the table top. It didn't take long to start thinking up another plan.

I was running out of time and I needed to be seated primly with my paper shirt wrapped around myself three times before Dr. Hart walked in. Time for drastic action. I climbed up on the foot rest at the end of the table, clung to the faux leather sides to prevent yet another fall, and crawled on my hands and knees to get to my desired location. I felt much like Sir Edmund Hillary must have felt when he reached the summit of Mt. Everest. After a few desperate attempts at straightening the paper toweling all bunched up under me, I gave up and wrapped my paper shirt around myself a few more times. At that moment Dr. Hart hobbled in and greeted his favorite patient.

So we were going through the usual questions – any recent trips to the hospital, any surgeries you haven't told me about, any falls? Well…let's talk about that one. Since Dr. Hart and I are old buddies, and he is better acquainted with my parts than I am, I started telling him – in ladylike terms – my little problem. He pushed and poked and thankfully he performed this from the back side so we didn't have to make eye contact.

And then he told me in medical terms that nothing is wrong with me, so just get over it. You know why he said that? Because it wasn't his busted butt. I would really like to sneak my folder out sometime and read his account of my appointment that day.

BARN QUILT

Dear Jennifer,

Our mountain county is really into barn quilts, probably because everybody in our mountain county has a barn. They might be living in a broken down mobile home propped up by concrete blocks and weighed down by old tires, but they have a nice barn in the back. Well, maybe not so nice, but the boards still hang together like a barn, so many of these barns are decorated with barn quilts. Our chamber of commerce even publishes barn quilt trail maps so you can enjoy a nice drive through the middle of nowhere looking at barn quilts.

Years ago I decided that my parents needed a barn quilt. For one thing, they already had everything else. For another, they had a barn. I knew they would never buy a barn quilt so I painted them one. A word to the wise: don't buy the supplies yourself unless you have a truck. While I did manage to convince the guys at the plywood store to cut this 4x8 piece of plywood into 2 4x4 pieces, they weren't about to carry them to my SUV, nor help me push, nudge, ram and cram them into the back. I might have torn a tiny hole in the lining because the 2 pieces just barely fit. Anyway, I painted a rather attractive barn quilt for them and surprised them both one Christmas. Those paint and primer coats made it that much more difficult to get the barn quilt into the back of my SUV. It was a very tight fit.

Fast forward to this year. Hubby has had a pole barn for 2 years now and he was embarrassed that he didn't have a barn quilt on his barn. This time I was smart. I made him go with me to the plywood store and he carried the 2 4x4 pieces to the truck and put them in there for me. This began in March. Since this was Hubby's barn quilt for Hubby's barn, Hubby got to choose the colors. This drove me nuts. You know Hubby is a computer guy. He let the computer help him pick his colors. This is where I say: "What am I, chopped liver?" But he insisted that the computer pick the colors, which it did.

I never thought I would be jealous of a computer. Naturally, I could only paint on the weekends, but after 4 months of preparation, I finally finished.

But now this barn quilt had to be hung and we don't have a ladder that high. Fortunately, the barn isn't a 2-story – it looks more like a garage – so Hubby had one of his engineer ideas. He parked his tractor just so, then raised the bucket as high as it would go. He climbed up the only ladder we have, stepped into the bucket and carefully balanced himself while my mom and I passed him this extremely awkward piece of plywood. It's hard enough to carry this thing across the floor, but to pass it up to Hubby made my arms want to scream. Visions of Moses holding his arms up during the battle against the Amalekites kept going through my mind. Moses had Aaron and Hur to support his tired arms. I only had my mom. Thank the Lord, Mom was there to help (she is going to take care of me when I get old).

Then we stood back and told Hubby to move it clockwise another inch, now counter-clockwise a half-inch. He was too close to the job to tell how far off he was with each adjustment. I didn't think he would ever get it right, but just as he was about to get irritated and settle for whatever position it was in, he finally nailed it. Technically, he screwed it up, but in a positive way. I have a great picture of him posing with his barn hanging equipment, partly to show the girls how their dad installed this barn quilt, and partly for photographic evidence to protect myself if he had fallen and I was blamed.

I have a 4x4 piece of plywood leftover and I think I'm going to paint a barn quilt for the side of the shed. This time, I get to choose the colors. And I'm not asking that silly computer for any input.

BIG FISH STORY

Dear Jennifer,

I got to visit with Sasquatch this past weekend. It's turkey hunting season and he was naturally hunting on our property. If it wasn't for his devotion to hunting and fishing, we would never see him. Also, we have the property that he likes to hunt on. Basically, he likes to hide behind our trees because his house is in town and he doesn't have trees to hide behind. And fortunately, or unfortunately, there is always something to hunt, so he is at our house all year long, we just don't see him hanging around that much. If nothing else is in season, he hunts coyotes because they are available every day of the year. I have learned more about hunting, hunting laws, hunting equipment, hunting places, hunting times, and hunting buddies than I ever thought possible. Don't think we don't like him hunting on our property. We really do. His massive presence is the best security system we ever had up there. Once he saw a stranger hunting on our land and ordered him off. Nobody argues with Sasquatch, especially the coyotes.

Sasquatch usually stops in for a friendly chat if we are home when he comes up - he does all the chatting. We just nod and smile. We could speak if we wanted to, but he is such a loquacious raconteur, it's much more entertaining if he does all the talking. It probably wouldn't surprise you to learn that several of us from that branch of the tree are gifted with loquacity. Anyway, he was telling us about his latest gun purchase. I wondered how many weapons he has. His dad offered to 'drive us through' Sasquatch's gun cabinet.

He showed me a picture of his latest new toy. How about that? A new gun. Correction: *another* new gun. Let's just say that his house is one that I will *never* break into no matter how hungry, broke or desperate I am.

But he wanted to brag on his fishing buddy that morning, not his new gun. His fishing buddy is his seven-year-old daughter.

We'll call her Sassy Squatch. She wears pink camo outfits and pink nail polish. Thank goodness, her mom still has some influence over her. Sasquatch took Sassy to his favorite fishin' hole. Sassy wore the proper fishing outfit for a seven-year-old girl and carried her Barbie rod and reel. They got to Sasquatch's secret fishing spot and he immediately saw a grass carp floating under the surface of the water. I don't know what a grass carp is, but its size must be impressive. Sasquatch showed Sassy the big fish. "I want to catch that one, Daddy," Sassy exclaimed with childlike innocence.

Sasquatch helped Sassy bait her hook with some sort of plastic squiggly lure. Sassy cast her Barbie rod - which kind of embarrasses me since I don't know how to do that - and started reeling her little squiggly lure in. She actually hooked the carp. Let's call it beginner's luck. Although Sassy is no stranger to fishing, she was a stranger to carp until that day. Sasquatch dropped his pole to give an assist, actually picking Sassy up, since the carp outweighed her. They put up a good fight until the carp broke Sassy's line. I guess the Barbie rod and reel set has a lower weight limit and was not designed to catch fish larger than guppies. It's probably a good thing that Sasquatch was holding onto Sassy. He probably had on too much fishing gear to actually jump in the water and chase after her and that fish as they swam up the river together.

The good news is, Sassy has a story to tell about the one that got away. But if your story starts out carp-sized at age seven, how do you go bigger?

Last fall Sassy told me that she and her dad had killed a deer and she was wondering when her dad was going to get around to field dressing it. That little kid is light years ahead of me in the hunting and fishing department. I console myself by thinking that Sassy probably can't do a vlookup in Excel yet.

TROUBLE AT THE WELL

Dear Jennifer,

It was the best of times. It was the worst of times. Saturday in the mountains was beautiful – low humidity, perfect temperature and not a cloud in the sky. Hubby and I saw a great blue heron fishing on the river. What a treat.

Hubby wanted his favorite blanket washed, so I threw it in the machine. I started washing and chopping veggies for roasting later in the day. I had bought ribeyes on sale the day before - first ribeyes in a year - and Hubby decided to grill his over an open fire for lunch. Everything was going smoothly. The washer was agitating, the fire was almost ready for a nice, juicy steak, I had just chopped up a turnip (for disciplinary purposes, not for enjoyment) and I turned on the faucet to wash the cauliflower. No water. Not a single drop. I immediately went into freak mode. Why wait until later? I like to freak at the very beginning and save time. The best of times was over.

I ran outside to Mr. Fixit. Hubby is my Super Hero in the 'broken things that need fixing department'. He can fix anything. If he doesn't know how to fix it, he will study it until he does know how to fix it. But at this moment, Hubby was ready to fix his delicious steak lunch, not water problems. So I had to wait for a few minutes. Then, after half an hour of examining the well and analyzing the data (math people always have to analyze data), hubby decided that he couldn't fix it. He actually had to call a professional plumber and leave a message to "please call us back, this is a top priority and my wife is in freak mode". While we waited, I felt that there was nothing else to do except turn to the stress basket. It had all the essentials: truffles, milk chocolate miniatures, and dark chocolate bars with sea salt caramel filling.

Then I remembered the blanket in the washer. This blanket is one of those faux fur things. They can hold 100 times their

120

weight in water. Probably. Now I know why certain people are called wet blankets. They put a real damper on things and you can't do a thing with them. The blanket was saturated; the washer had not reached the spin cycle yet and it wasn't designed for people in freak mode to advance the button to the next cycle. Just my luck. I got a kitchen garbage bag, the 13-gallon size, and attempted to wring the water out of the blanket into the washer as I slowly stuffed wet *heavy*, somewhat wrung out faux fur into the bag. This took some time and no, Hubby couldn't help me. He was waiting for the plumber to call back and his cell doesn't have service inside the house (this can be a real drag on a rainy January evening), so he had to stand outside and wait for me to bring him his wet blanket. He had a plan for getting it dry.

I finally had the garbage bag stuffed with wet blanket, but I buy the cheap store brand bags, not the name brand kind that can hold a baby grand, so the bag began to tear as I tried to lift it. It was too heavy to lift anyway. It weighed 400 pounds. Fortunately, I was able to pull and push it onto the bathroom rug and eventually, there was enough bagged wet blanket on the rug to be able to pull the rug outside and find out Hubby's plan for the drying process. This plan involved spreading the blanket across the truck bed so the sun could do the work. Working as a team - we were the Dry Team - we hoisted the blanket onto the truck bed and Hubby started spreading it out as I wrung out more water. After 15 minutes of squeezing out gallons of water by hand, we weren't the Dry Team anymore. Thank goodness it wasn't cold outside. And we have had to thaw pipes down at that well in 9° weather in the dark with a hair dryer, so I wasn't complaining about that part.

Those sweet plumbers (there were 2 of them) spent 9 hours at our house. And since I consider this man's work, I stayed inside and read cozy mysteries and took naps for most of that time. We all deal with stress in our own way. My way is with chocolate and books. I couldn't really do anything else. I might have gotten dirty and I wouldn't be able to wash my hands. Hubby spent the entire time outside with those boys and tried to be as helpful as he could. When we were finally presented with the bill for a new well pump (and the 2 plumbers and I picked Hubby up off the floor), the senior plumber – I think he was 19 – told me confidentially that they had to charge more because Hubby helped them so much.

HILLBILLY LABOR DAY

Dear Jennifer,

Labor Day weekend. You know what that means: Hillbilly Jamboree at the family campground. The northern kin arrived Friday before we did. This trip included wives which made it a lot more pleasant for me. Even Mrs. Sasquatch was there. She usually stays home and enjoys the peace and quiet. I love my cousins dearly, but there's only so much huntin' and fishin' talk I can endure. Sometimes it's more interesting if 'the big one that got away' is a purse I saw on sale and waited too late to buy it. Occasionally, I caught a break between big fish stories and asked about the grandchildren. Occasionally, a wife caught a break between 9-point buck stories and answered me back.

On Saturday Hubby wanted to take the campers some firewood. With the help of his trusty tractor, Hubby dragged some of our fallen trees down to the campground. My job was to watch the chains wrapped around the tree trunks and get Hubby's attention if something was amiss. This was no big deal. I was walking slowly behind the tractor as it inched down the driveway pulling dead trees.

What I hadn't counted on was that the trees were moving down the driveway faster than I was, and as they neared, they were taking up more driveway space as the slim trunks gave way to outstretched limbs. I was suddenly faced with a decision: get dragged down the driveway wrapped up in dead tree branches, do a tuck and roll off the side of the driveway and down the embankment, or remember my gymnastics class from 1970. I chose to remember gymnastics and gave myself a 10 for the perfect vault I performed over some pretty scratchy-looking branches. It's amazing what desperation can make one do. Maybe if my P.E. teacher had used a tractor and tree branches I could've made an A in gymnastics class. This wasn't the junior high P.E. teacher who had me Moron-listed. This was my high school P.E. teacher. And she might have thought I was a moron, but she was too nice to say it.

The trees made it safely down to the campground, only holding up traffic on our little one-lane road for a couple of minutes. A driver hauling a canoe trailer had to sit and watch the trees cross the road, but as he was probably getting paid by the hour, he didn't seem to mind too much.

When Hubby dropped his load by the fire Cousin Fergus whipped out his trusty chainsaw – he never leaves home without it – and went through all those trunks and branches like a hot knife through butter. We say that a lot up in the mountains.

Later, as we sat around the campfire enjoying the peaceful New River and the beauty of carefully stacked firewood, Sasquatch wanted me to tell Fergus about how I write you stories about him. "Hey, Cuz, tell Fergus how you write to that lady about me." He loves being the center of attention at family gatherings and he practically glowed when I told him that he is the subject of some of the tales I send you. I haven't sent you a fraction of the Sasquatch stories I have on file. Maybe someday I'll write his biography, only I think a biography is supposed to be mostly true stuff. Sasquatch would want me to add things that probably couldn't physically happen, like the college football story he told at the campground Saturday. He caught the ball, ran 98 yards with it in his arms, and carried 2 opposing players on his back. A third opposing player took him down at the 2-yard line by grabbing his legs, but Sasquatch was able to shove the ball over the goal line and score however many points you get for a touchdown. And he was only 8 years old.

It still might be interesting to add to his biography. Paul Bunyan was bigger than life and he had a biography. Or maybe it was a tall tale. Practically the same thing where Sasquatch is concerned.

MASK ADVANTAGES

Dear Jennifer,

I was at the grocery store Saturday and was halfway finished with my shopping when I realized I had forgotten my mask. I wondered why people were giving me dirty looks, although several of them were pushing their carts the wrong way against those large yellow arrows on the floor. I should have returned their dirty looks, but I am a sweetie and have better behavior than that. Anyway, I was panicking about my mask. It has become a regular accessory, like earrings, purse and shoes, so I was struggling with this. I went back to the meat department, grabbed a paper towel, and tucked it gently between my lips. I looked like I was blotting an enormous lipstick error. Walking around the store became a challenge because the paper towel was bigger than my face which is where I keep my eyes, so I sort of had to walk sideways like a crab so I could shop without banging the cart into the ham hocks rack or the frozen shrimp bin. That probably should have been made into 2 sentences. I got a new variety of looks after this but they weren't dirty anymore – curious is probably the best description. I suppose most people have never shopped in the same store with a person whose entire face is behind a square paper towel.

As annoying as it is to wear this mask, wash it, remember to put it back in my purse and whip it out in any public place, I have discovered that it does have its advantages. For one thing, it hides my nose. When I'm going for a dental visit or a hair appointment, I always give myself a final nose check before I leave my car. No one wants to see bats in the cave. So I went to see Lana Nichols this week, wearing my mask, but I forgot to do the final nose check. While my head was tilted back getting the best shampoo in the world – Lana has magic fingers - her retinas were safe because my mask was covering whatever it might have been that I forgot to do a search and pick for.

Another advantage of the mask is that if I have spinach between my teeth, I'm covered. You have no idea how often I unintentionally store a little piece of spinach between my teeth. And it never resides in the back - no, it likes to hang out front where it is more noticeable. Once, we went to a fancy dinner for scholarship winners at App State. Guess what was on my salad? Right. After the fancy dinner, the chancellor got up to speak, so I had to look interested. He opened with a cute little joke - I think an opening joke is required in public speaking - and I smiled politely. Bea looked at me. Isn't it funny how when two or more people hear something funny, they immediately look at someone else to see if they are laughing? Is this an insecurity thing? So Bea looked at me. And instead of sharing a smile with me like two people are supposed to do when the speaker says something funny and one turns to look at the other for security purposes, Bea had a look of horror on her face. Her gaze was directed toward my teeth. I knew immediately what was wrong.

Bea and I have worked out a wordless communication system over the years, so she began trying to communicate which two teeth I needed to start digging between. After a few failed attempts - I said that we have worked out a wordless communication system; I didn't say it is 100% effective - Bea got the silly giggles. Fortunately, the chancellor was still giving his opening remarks, keeping it light and humorous. I guess. I was pretty busy at the moment and didn't have time to pay attention to his little speech. Unfortunately, several professors were sitting at our table and Bea wanted to make a good impression. At that time, she wasn't sure if she would be in their particular classes and didn't want to get started off on the wrong foot. I finally got smart and excused myself to go to the ladies' room. I had to make a digging tool out of a folded paper towel. Thank goodness, they didn't have those hot air hand dryers in there. I would have looked pretty ridiculous sticking my head under that thing and *blowing* the spinach out from between my teeth. The spinach was wedged in there pretty well and several ladies, pretending to wash their hands, kept staring at me and trying not to be obvious about it. They probably never have spinach between their teeth. Well, now they know how to deal with it if it ever happens.

I certainly didn't mean to take up all this space discussing spinach. I don't even like it that much. And if I come across more advantages to wearing the mask, you will be the first to know.

FOOD MISHAPS

Dear Jennifer,

Some of our neighbors got together and decided we needed to have our first ever block party. Our neighborhood has been in existence for 22 years. I'm not sure what prompted this sudden need for a block party. But Hubby and I were all in and wanted to participate. It was going to be nice to meet some of the neighbors we haven't known for 22 years.

A very generous neighbor volunteered the hamburgers, hotdogs and chicken, and the rest of us were supposed to bring a side dish. We were planning to be in the mountains until the day of, so I had to come up with something ahead of time that would keep. My marinated slaw is the perfect recipe for just such an event. It is delicious all by itself or with hamburgers and hot dogs and it keeps for weeks. That is the best advertisement for slaw I ever heard. So I made it the week before the party. I gave it a little stir each day so that it would be perfect. I only see my neighbors on those rare occasions when I actually walk in our neighborhood, so it was important that they like my food since they probably think I'm a stuck-up snob.

Hubby and I left the cabin on Saturday and got home just in time to brush our teeth, and grab our lawn chairs and required side dish. Everything was moving like clockwork. We were on schedule and were going to have some fun with our neighbors.

Hubby picked up the lawn chairs and I picked up my huge Tupperware bowl full of slaw and dropped it on the porch. Just like that. Dropped it. Slaw sounds sort of like 'schplock' when landing on pressure treated wood. I just stood there in shock.

Let me reiterate that I made this slaw IN ADVANCE so I would be prepared. I stirred it every night so the flavors would marry. This was the mother of all slaws. So I stood there while

Hubby hosed down the rug, the floor and me. (The slaw had a lot of oil and vinegar in it).

So we showed up at the block party late (and last) and I showed up wet. There hadn't been any time left to change into dry clothes after my oil and vinegar rinse. And we showed up with half of a huge Tupperware bowl full of slaw. The food was good, the conversation flowed. I sat there in a snit. My next door neighbor raved about my slaw. He went back for seconds. So I told him if he really liked it, there was more in the back yard.

But there's more …

We have an old fridge in our garage, which is pretty handy. It's basically a large Coke machine. But it is very useful for holiday food overflow and also for holding the perishables I plan to take to the cabin each trip. Hubby sees them sitting there and knows exactly what to pack in the cooler. That way the truck is loaded and waiting for me to jump in when it's time to leave. It's a process he and I have perfected over the years and it's really great, because Hubby does all the work and I just get in the truck.

So last night I got home from the grocery store, unloaded the groceries, and sorted out the things I needed to take to the cabin this weekend. I piled up an armload of perishables and I could tell that they were not balanced safely in my arms. I suffer from lazy girl syndrome, which means I always try to take everything in one trip. This almost always gets me into trouble and I almost always regret not making two trips, yet I continue to behave the same way each time, hoping for a different outcome.

Sure enough, when I got to the top step going down into the garage, the hummus slipped off the yogurt and hit the bricks. I had just tasted it and it was the best flavor I ever bought – everything hummus, just like the everything bagel. I couldn't drop the nasty yogurt. No, I had to drop the hummus, which was $4.49 and still cold from the store. If only I hadn't opened it for a sample taste, things wouldn't have gone so far south so quickly.

Hummus hitting the bricks sounds a lot like slaw hitting porch wood: schplock. Next challenge: cleaning it off. Using a plastic spoon, I scraped off all I could, but brick has nooks and crannies. Paper towels and a wet rag followed. The bricks actually looked better before they were hit with the paper towels. Before, they were stained with hummus, which was close to the same color. After wiping vigorously with paper towels, there were thousands of little white paper crumbs on the bricks. The only thing going for me was that the nights are cooler now, so maybe the bugs are gone. If I were a bug, that's where I would hang out.

But wait, we aren't finished …

I had a rare day last weekend which didn't require housework or office work or much of anything else. It was a perfect time to sip hot tea, read a good mystery (Agatha Christie's *The Moving Finger*) and cuddle up in my big chair with a blankie.

But I needed a cookie to complete my perfect weekend. A cup of Earl Grey is always that much better with a cookie. I expected to have trouble finding a good low cholesterol cookie recipe. What would I do without Google? I would starve to death, for one thing. But I found a pretty good recipe. I can usually taste the ingredients in my mind, so I was pretty sure this was the real deal. To be perfectly honest, I try not to taste flour in my mind; just the good stuff. The recipe was called 'Lower My Cholesterol Oatmeal Cookies'. That had my name written all over it.

I went to the fridge for the eggs (egg whites only in this recipe), but something was rotten in Denmark. I didn't need Agatha Christie to help me solve this mystery. There was a plastic tub in the back (where all the bad food goes to hide) and it had half of a tomato in it. Probably from 2012, I couldn't be sure. It was so nasty I couldn't even save my plastic tub. I took the whole thing out to the trash can. Since I was in too much of a rush to have my cookie, tea and mystery combo with blankie on the side, I chose not to walk down the 4 steps to the trash. I simply gave the plastic tub a gentle toss into the can. It wasn't very far and my aim is pretty good where trash is concerned. Most of the time. When a rotten tomato is involved, I should know better. I almost made a 2-point shot (maybe it could have been a 3-point shot – I don't know what the rules are regarding tomato sports), but it bounced off the rim. The plastic tub landed in the paint and the tomato and plastic lid went out of bounds. Perhaps I should have attempted a goal tending maneuver before it was too late.

FYI - rotten tomatoes make a bit of a splash. All the time I wanted to save by giving the plastic tub a toss, was multiplied exponentially on the waste of time side. I rinsed and scrubbed and sniffed, checking for any tomato splats that might be hiding behind SUV tires. Don't try to picture me on my hands and knees on the garage floor doing a bloodhound routine. It isn't pretty. Now there is a really clean circle on the garage floor, except where the red tomato stains are. It sort of resembles the planet Jupiter. You would think something as hard as concrete wouldn't be so porous.

Now it was time for the fun part - making my cookie dough. I seriously needed to make up for lost time. I cracked an egg, separated it, and dropped the white into the large mixing bowl. I cracked the second egg. I shouldn't crack an egg so enthusiastically on a granite surface. That was a different sort of egg separation. I separated the shell from the egg and all of it was on the countertop. The good news is that broken eggs are a lot easier to clean up than tomato explosions. You can sort of slide those babies right into the trash can. I cracked egg #3 a little more carefully, and managed to separate it successfully and drop the white into the large mixing bowl.

It was time to measure flour and I was most seriously behind schedule. I had a brand new 5-pound bag of flour and needed to empty it into my flour canister. Really, I've been around long enough to know to expect some things to simply happen. I should, but somehow, I still forget to remind myself that kitchen mishaps follow me around like a shadow. Funny thing about flour: it just seems to float everywhere like a dusty cloud. It was on the countertop, on every cookie making utensil lying on the countertop, in the cracks of the floor. I was not loving a hardwood floor in the kitchen at this time. This is the hardwood floor with beveled edges on each piece of wood that the really good hardwood floor salesman talked us into buying. Beveled edges make a beautiful floating flour trap.

At this point, I should probably rate clean-up for future reference.

Easiest: raw eggs. An egg seems to want to hang together, so you can clean it fairly quickly.
Moderate: flour. It creates flurries, but it's dry and can be vacuumed up, if necessary.
Impossible: rotten tomato. It simply goes everywhere, especially in a garage. You have to crawl under the car, into far corners where only vermin go, and touch things that little old ladies shouldn't have to touch.

Back to the kitchen. I didn't mess up the important part. I made 3 dozen delicious low cholesterol oatmeal raisin cookies. Even though my mind is aware that there is no butter in these cookies, it still sent the message to my stomach that these are really, really good and I can have 3 cookies at a time.

In my opinion, I have always been a pretty good cook. I've never bragged about being a neat one. And although I can't blame anyone but myself for the slaw and hummus casualties, Earl Grey and Agatha Christie are purely to blame for the cookie disaster. If they hadn't rushed me so, I would've taken my time and done the job without all those accidents.

KILLER, THE PIT BULL

Dear Jennifer,

Cousin Fergus and one of his huntin' buddies came in for the Thanksgiving weekend. Since we weren't formally introduced, I'll call him Thurmond. My cousins never heard of Emily Post. There are never introductions. You are supposed to pick up any personal information you need in the conversations you overhear. Like: "me an' ole Thurmond here got us a box o' cartridges". So I figured his name was Thurmond.

Joining Fergus and Thurmond were several of the other cousins – all males. And Killer, the pit bull. For some reason, my cousins never go anywhere without their dogs. It may go back to the days when our families made their own moonshine and the dogs were there to sound a warning if the revenuers got too close.

The guys were having a really good time, and based on the total number of cans (the empties plus the as yet unconsumed), a couple of beer companies will have a good 4th quarter this year. There was a big bonfire going (which was great because I was freezing to death) and Johnny Cash was singing on the radio which was propped on an enormous cooler.

The guys were doing a little skeet shooting over the river. No one lives on the other side, so the local citizens were safe. Killer the pit bull didn't like those loud guns and was cowering in the cab of a pickup truck. I said Killer is a pit bull. I didn't say Killer is a *fearless* pit bull. When she saw me, she jumped out of the truck, ran over to our golf cart, and jumped in my lap. I didn't realize that our relationship had progressed to that level. She usually barks at me for at least a half hour. I must have appeared to be a safe haven amidst all those rough men and guns, or I was giving off a granny aura. Now we're buddies.

She snuggled up as close to me as she could get, which was

alright because she had body heat. I was freezing to death and Sasquatch had on shorts and clogs. Every time a gun went off, Killer snorted dog snot on my jacket sleeve. Good thing it's the green jacket.

Hubby and I visited the cousins for a while, and then said our goodbyes. On pretty days we cruise down the river road in the golf cart and enjoy the scenery. We're not usually so fortunate as to have pretty days in November so we took advantage of the beautiful weather. Hubby and I left the campground and headed down the river road with Killer between us. She and I had bonded. She was stuck to my side like fleas on a … well, you know.

She rode the entire mile down to the end of the road and back, sniffing new smells in the air. I sensed that she was having a good time. She didn't say anything. Hubby was having fun also. He has always wanted a weekend dog. We don't have time for a full time dog. So Killer was sort of our Rent-A-Dog. As we approached the campground she jumped out and ran back to her daddy. The ride back to the cabin was a lot colder without her beside me.

Arriving at the cabin, I attacked my jacket with a lint roller to remove all those dog hairs. Very unattractive. And I'll just bet that next time Killer sees me she'll bark her head off, forgetting how I saved her from those scary noises the other day.

CHAINSAW

Dear Jennifer,

Last Saturday morning was perfect - low humidity, soft breeze, just a little hint of fall in the Blue Ridge. The perfect day to winterize the camper, then move it down to the barn. We opened the camper door, the water heater lid, and the back storage bay lid. Then we heard a little crack. We looked at each other and said "Did you hear that? It sounded like a little crack". We are so expressive. We worked a few more minutes and heard another little crack. Then we did some serious staring into the tree limbs, all of which seem to lean over the shed and aim toward the cabin, and all of which are huge, old, and soar about 75 feet. Is it that one? Could it be that one? Then there was another crack and this time, there was no mistaking the sound or its location. It was the big limb hanging right over the truck.

And I thought Hubby couldn't run fast. He dove into the truck just as I heard a very loud crack and all I could think of was that some limbs are referred to as widow makers. Hubby put that truck in R and backed that baby out of there at about 60 mph (that's pretty fast going backwards). He got out of the truck and then we watched and heard the very large limb just sort of ease itself on down to the ground, taking the top halves of 3 other trees with it. We did what we have done about 7 other times this year: stood there and stared at it, thinking AGAIN? In China, 2020 is the year of the Rat. In our family, it's the year of Fallen Trees.

So we closed the back storage bay lid, the water heater lid, and the camper door, put on our go to town clothes, and drove to the hardware store to buy a chainsaw. After numerous downed trees this year, we decided that when it happens at home the chainsaw is in the mountains, and vice versa. At this rate, a permanent chainsaw at the cabin seemed like a good investment.

We brought our new chainsaw home and were unboxing it when a vehicle pulled up. Oh boy, our neighbor cousins heard the noise and brought chainsaws and fried chicken. Well a girl can dream, can't she? It was a couple of Bea's friends spending the day looking for mountain property and they had stopped by to meet us. Not a good day to meet me when I had on my sawdust outfit and smelled like I had worn it a really long time. Plus, my hair was full of twigs and branches. My head looked like an enormous bird's nest. Then those clean, well dressed strangers wanted a tour of the cabin. It was never messier.

At that point I remembered a line I always quote from a John Lennon song: Life is what happens while you're busy making other plans.

But help was just around the corner. Cousin Fergus was in for the weekend. And guess what he always brings with him on vacation? His chainsaw. I bring my Kindle when I take a trip. We're different that way. Cousin Fergus brought Mrs. Cousin Fergus this time. She wanted a tour of the cabin. It. Was. Never. Messier. Why was this the weekend for tours? Life is just funny that way. Unless it is your messy house everybody wants to see. Then life isn't all that funny – it's embarrassing.

Cousin Fergus is a professional tree cutter and choreographed the felling of broken trees like nothing I ever saw. I even filmed it. Poetry in motion. And he wouldn't take any money. He also hauled away 4 truckloads of wood for the family campground. Now we just have to spend a few days picking up branches. And picking twigs out of my hair.

The unexpected surprise was that Bea's friends became our friends. They found some mountain property near our cabin and we have been over to visit several times. You just never know what's going to happen when you are making other plans.

EARLY BIRD SHOPPER

Dear Jennifer,

Have you put up your tree yet? We started Sunday. I strung the lights from bottom to top - or started out that way. I actually went from bottom to a third of the way up because I ran out of lights. We looked all over the house and couldn't find any more. Then we remembered that last year when we took all the decorations down we threw out all the lights that half worked. We even said that we would forget to replace them before next Christmas.

And we did forget, so we had a third of a tree lit for all the passersby to enjoy, scratch their heads, and wonder what sort of decorating theme we were going for. I planned a trip to buy more lights.

In December I avoid the store AND the main road into town like the plague. I was driving to work Monday morning, dreading the very thought of creeping along the main road after work, sitting at each red light through three light changes, and elbowing my way through the store to the Christmas section. Then it hit me: the store is open 24/7. So at 5:47 a.m. I whipped my car into the store's parking lot, parked at the garden center door (which is where the Christmas stuff is) and approached.

For future reference - the garden center door is open only during 'normal' business hours. So I got back in my car, drove a half mile to the real open door, and walked in. I grabbed my cart - the one with the square wheel in the back, and walked all the way to the Christmas department in the garden center, which was as far as I could get from the real open door. The square wheel in the back of the cart assured every stock boy in the store that I wasn't sneaking around. But it was okay, because it really was just me and all the stock boys. Shopper's heaven: no sharing of space. The store was entirely mine. Too bad I didn't desperately need anything else.

Suddenly I was overcome with an irresistible urge to shop because the store was mine, all mine. I bought bread, cookies, a couple of new potholders and a switch plate for the guestroom. I picked up some beef jerky – I can't wait to try this because I've never tasted it – moth balls, and 2 pairs of socks. There were vitamins in the pharmacy and dental floss and shampoo. I left the mustache trimmer on the shelf because I couldn't think of a single person who might need one, except Aunt Dorothea, but we don't exchange gifts and she might think I expect her to buy me something equally useful next year. I found a pretty shower curtain and some picture frames and some nice towels. All these great deals were going into my cart until it was full and overflowing. And why did I buy all these things? Because I could and because nobody was in my way.

The cashier was awfully glad to see me; she just didn't know how to show it. It took her a little while to ring up all my purchases. And it took me a little while to get all that stuff loaded into the back of my car. I was exhausted when I finally returned my empty cart to the stand and sat back in the driver's seat. Just as I was about to turn the key in the ignition it hit me: the Christmas lights.

I ran back to the real open door, all the way back to the garden center, grabbed six boxes of lights, ran all the way back to the other end of the store, scanned them at the self-check (the cashier had seen me coming and ducked behind the register), and I was finally on my way to work at 6:30. I was exhausted, but I got a really good workout.

Now I have calmed down somewhat and am wondering: do you need any mothballs?

BEA'S WHITE SWEATSUIT

Dear Jennifer,

I was eating lunch with Phyllis in the cafeteria the other day when she dropped a blob of spaghetti on her shirt. We never have gotten through an entire lunch without one of us staining a shirt; it just usually doesn't happen so quickly into the lunch hour. Naturally, this reminds me of a story.

Bea always had a thing about a new outfit. Every time she had something new to wear, she insisted on wearing it that very day. And invariably, she always dropped something on it at supper time. And invariably, that something was always a tomato-based food.

Bea and Ellen were required to have white sweatsuits for the Christmas play at church. They were going to be angels in the Angel Brigade. I bought 2 pretty white sweatsuits and put them aside for the play. Bea begged for weeks to be allowed to wear her sweatsuit to school. I had been through enough tomato-based laundry projects to know better than to allow this. I promised her that as soon as the play was over, she could wear her pretty white sweatsuit to school.

The Christmas play was a big hit and the girls played their parts very well. I will brag a little here and say that they both had important speaking and singing parts and did a wonderful job. They got their ham DNA from my side of the family.

Naturally, Bea was planning to wear her white sweatsuit to school the very next day. I got a call at the office around 10:00 that morning. The class had gone outside for recess; Bea had found a huge rock, thrown it into the creek and splashed mud all over her white sweatsuit. Could I please bring a change of clothes? I went home, grabbed a clean outfit, including socks, shoes and undies because I knew my little girl very well, and headed for school.

When I got to the classroom, everything stopped. All Bea's little classmates looked at me, then at Bea. She was covered in mud from hair to shoes. I still can't figure out how she could lift a rock heavy enough to make such a splash. What a sad sorrowful little face looked back at me. Words were not needed. I had made my point, or rather, Bea had made it for me. Lucky for her that I brought extra undies. That's another head scratcher. How did mud find its way all the way in there? Needless to say, that sweatsuit was never worn again. North Carolina clay doesn't wash out of whites very well.

Bea got her ham DNA from me, but she got her mud DNA from Hubby. When he was just about the same age, he was wearing white pants one Sunday. It had been raining and there were patches of mud in the yard. While their parents were still getting ready for church, Hubby and his big brother Fred were out in the yard. Fred told Hubby to see how fast he could run around the house. Little Hubby made it around the house in 15 seconds. Fred told him to see if he could go faster. Little Hubby made it around the house in 14.5 seconds. Fred told him to try once more to see if he could go any faster. The third time around it took little Hubby 2 minutes and 30 seconds to get all the way around because he had finally hit the mud puddle that Fred had been aiming him at on the previous 2 laps. On Hubby's 60th birthday, Fred gave him a picture of the 2 of them. Hubby was wearing his white pants. That must have been the last time they looked good.

I think Hubby and Bea both learned a lesson on their respective mud days. Hubby learned to not trust people if he happened to be wearing white on a rainy day. Bea learned to not trust herself if she happened to be wearing white on any kind of day.

THE GIFTS ARE ALL WRAPPED

Dear Jennifer,

Today is my second favorite day of the year. My topmost first best favorite day of the year is Winter Solstice day. After that, the days start getting longer. It's not so bleak outside, plus I'm afraid of the dark a little less each day. Naturally, my worst, most unfavorite day of the year is Summer Solstice day. When the days start getting shorter, I get just a tad bit sad. And I start getting afraid of the dark earlier each day.

But today is All The Christmas Gifts Are Finally Wrapped Day. I hate wrapping gifts, mainly because I am so bad at it. The only person worse than I am at gift wrapping is Hubby. One time he bought me a camera and tried to wrap it all by himself. It took two hours, half a roll of tape and an entire brand new roll of wrapping paper. I'll never understand how he took so long, or wasted so much paper. He did have an excuse though – he had never wrapped a gift before that day. I have wrapped hundreds, maybe thousands of gifts. They all end up the same way: bunched up on the ends with too much give in the middle. It's like every box shrinks after I wrap it – sort of how I looked when I was in Weight Watchers and went down two sizes and my jeans kept slipping off. That was embarrassing. But that's another story.

Last month I was at the big box store and bought a large roll of very pretty paper. Not only was this paper pretty, it was reversible, and sensibly priced. So I decided to wrap female gifts with one side of the paper and male gifts with the other. That was my third mistake.

My first mistake was trying to wrap my gifts on the bedroom floor. I was trying to break my habit of waiting until Christmas Eve and thought I could watch a corny Christmas movie while I wrapped a few gifts. It wasn't very comfortable but it was handy and I wasn't messing up the living room with little bits of paper scraps. I sat in the lotus position for so long, my back went out. That was a week ago and my back still hurts. Not to worry, according to the internet it is only a sprain and I will get over it eventually. Where would we be without WebMD?

My second mistake was moving my gift wrapping assembly to the dining room. Now another room was messy with bits of paper scraps. But it was more comfortable to stand at the table and wrap. I thought. The problem was that this large roll of box store paper was 350 square feet and weighed at least 40 pounds. I could gift wrap a bus with this roll of paper. So it was a little cumbersome. I was in the dining room with a perfectly large surface to wrap gifts on, except that half the surface of the table was covered with gift tags, empty gift boxes, gifts waiting to be wrapped, and a tape dispenser. Somewhere.

Remember: one side of the paper for male gifts (mostly blue with silver Christmas trees) and the other side of the paper for female gifts (mostly white with FaLaLaLaLa in several shades of blue). Things were going reasonably well. I heaved the 40 pound roll of paper onto the table, unrolled it as far to the edge of the table as I thought was safe, and placed a large gift on the paper, leaving just enough margin to cover the sides. Now I was ready to cut. But I let the roll go to reach for the scissors, and it kept rolling. Off the table edge, banging against the chair at the end of the table, and bouncing onto the floor. And ripping up a perfectly good seven foot length of gift wrap. Time for a new strategy: shoving the debris to the opposite end of the table to give myself more room before I start unrolling. I began again. This time the paper was cut, I wrapped the gift as I always do – like a butcher wraps a roast. Slapped the to-from tag on there, then realized I had wrapped a male gift with the female side of the paper.

When Christmas is stressful enough, why do I find it necessary to add to the pressure by color coordinating the gifts? And why didn't I call Eloise to help me in the first place? The remainder of the gifts got wrapped with whatever side of the paper was up at the time, and nobody will ever know what my silly plan was. After I had wrapped most of the gifts and figured the weight of the roll of paper was down somewhat, I decided it was time to wrap the big gift that was about the height of four stacked dining room chairs, since that is what was in the box. Time to get creative. The box was too heavy to move and besides, my back was hurting, so I thought 'outside the box'. The box sat still and I ran around it, unrolling the paper as I went. Piece of cake. And several pieces of tape. Anyway, all the gifts are wrapped now and I have stopped cringing when I see Jarrod's basketball with Ellen's gift wrap on it.

COVID CHRISTMAS

Dear Jennifer,

Our family always has a huge Christmas brunch on the Saturday before Christmas. The martyr in me sacrifices Christmas with my children so that they can be with their in-laws on Christmas Day. I think that's pretty big of me, plus it gets me in good with my sons-in-law. Someday I hope to win the 'Mother-in-law of the Year' award. I have been in the running for it several times, or at least I should have been.

We have a huge meal - eggs, bacon, sausage, fruit, biscuits, muffins, desserts, and a grits bar. The grits bar satisfies the hillbilly in each of us. Ellen is in charge of the grits bar. She brings a large crock pot full of grits and has toppings on the side. It's awesome. I have a hot drinks bar with coffee, tea and spiced apple cider.

After we have eaten until we're sick, we read the Christmas story and sing Christmas carols. By this time the grandkids are worked up to a fever pitch and are about to bust wanting their presents. We purposely make it last just to irritate them. But we also remind them that anticipation makes it more fun.

Last week Ellen brought the kids over for a visit and they made a beeline for the tree. I had the presents all neatly stacked under the tree to make room for as many gifts as I could. I don't even put bows on my packages so that I can cram more stuff under there. They started taking inventory. Athena came and reported to me that she had three presents and Hawkins only had two presents. After a few minutes, Hawkins wanted me to know that he also had three presents under the tree. Isn't that cute? To give me an inventory as if I didn't know the exact location of every single package?

Anyway, our house is wild and crazy the Saturday before Christmas and it's a lot of fun for everybody.

Except for this year. Thank you, Covid.

This year is a total bust. The best we can do is truck their presents over to their homes, then meet on Zoom so that we can at least watch Athena and Hawkins (and Cedric, Julius and Belle) open those three presents.

ZOOM CHRISTMAS

Dear Jennifer,

Our Zoom Virtual Christmas was a bit of a challenge. We didn't have enough band width at the cabin to see the kids open presents, so we took a laptop and an iPad to the Burger Barn in town. They have free WiFi there. In theory. We opened the back doors of the truck and took out everything that wasn't bolted on at the factory and put it all in my front seat. I'm not sure why there is so much stuff back there, but I have been informed that it is all necessary stuff. Then we put the iPad on the console which acted as our tabletop, and started trying to get onto Burger Barn's free WiFi. We spent about 20 minutes trying to get their WiFi to kick in and it didn't happen. Another 20 minutes on the laptop. Nope. Maybe the manager saw us out in the parking lot and wouldn't let us use their free WiFi for free.

There we were sitting in the back seat of a red pickup truck, when a sheriff's car pulled up beside us. How embarrassing. Fortunately, it was only Sasquatch, checking for hanky panky offenders. Us? We were the oldest people in the parking lot. Shoot! *We are older than the parking lot.* We are even older than the Burger Barn. When we told Sasquatch our plans to watch the kids open presents, he decided it was his break time. He scooched in between us so he could get a good seat. In the cozy back seat of our truck. The back seat where my knees hit the back of the front seat. It's that tight back there. I still don't know where he put his knees while he was back there. We were so snug, I think the impression of the door handle is still in my side. The free WiFi not working turned out to be a blessing. Virtual Christmas is one thing. Virtual breathing is quite another. This reminded me of one of my trips out to Kansas City. I was in the middle seat in a hot plane when a rather large man, who should have been charged for two seats, sat next to me in the aisle seat. Obviously, he traveled quite a bit because he had no qualms about resting his beefy left arm on top of my bony right arm for the duration of the flight and looked like he was used to sharing seats with his fellow passengers. In disgust, I looked at the skinny guy on the other side of me and he said, "Well, it has to go *some*where."

Anyway, we were thinking about any other possible options when Hubby remembered that he had USB tethering on the cheap phone we only use when we're in the mountains. I don't know what that means – I hope you do. So we wedged ourselves out of the back seat, said 'good-bye' to Sasquatch, took everything out of the front seat and put it in the back again, then drove back home to get set up. So far, we had wasted an hour and a half to get nowhere. Then we hooked up the tether phone and it wouldn't work from the cabin. This whole virtual Christmas thing was losing its appeal. Jarrod told us to get the Zoom app on a cell phone. Seriously? It won't work on an iPad, a laptop, or USB tethering, whatever that is, and you actually think our cell phone will work? Well, it did. We finally got to see our kiddos on the smallest screen in the universe, but the important thing was we could see them.

But Hubby wasn't finished. He downloaded a screen share app and the picture popped up on our TV. The great big TV. The largest piece of furniture in our cabin. It was finally Christmas. Jed played my Zoom Christmas song on his cigar box guitar and Bea sang. We were all moved. A few moved right out of the room. Jed makes guitars out of cigar boxes and gave each of Ellen's three children a cigar box guitar. They were thrilled. That house was so noisy with all those budding guitarists, it was like watching all the Whoville children celebrating Christmas with their jingtinglers and trumtookas. We were beginning to think that virtual isn't so bad sometimes. With virtual Christmas, you can actually turn the kids' volume down.

So glad that we didn't spend all 3.5 hours of our Zoom Christmas in the Burger Barn parking lot. We would have frozen to death and could not have taken those occasional bathroom breaks. And we would be permanently bonded to Sasquatch. We would be billed as the world's first Siamese triplets. Actually, if the Burger Barn free WiFi had worked, I suppose the free bathrooms would have been available also. I might have ordered a double cheeseburger out of guilt - I can't say for sure. And also medium fries.

CHRISTMAS IN THE MOUNTAINS

Dear Jennifer,

Hubby and I decided to spend Christmas in the mountains this year. We had already 'zoomed' with the kiddos, so there didn't seem to be much point in hanging around an empty house. Having heard the weather report many times last week, we figured that extra groceries might not hurt if we got snowed in. While we were in our small town grocery store we ran into Cousin Junior and the beautiful, glamorous Mrs. Cousin Junior. FYI - If you ever decide to live in a small town, always look decent when you go out. You never know when you'll run into kin.

I got up to the checkout and was unloading the groceries onto the belt, picked up a package of blueberries and suddenly there was an explosion in my hand. Blueberries flew all over the store. It looked like blue fireworks. I was picking up blueberries all across the front of the store alone – ask me how many shoppers stood around NOT helping me pick up blueberries. I was hoping Mrs. Cousin Junior wouldn't see me (she is extremely classy) - when Hubby came up to the counter and explained to the cashier how sorry he was. He had only left me unattended for a minute. So embarrassing. He also stepped on berries or rolled over them with the grocery cart every time he moved. There was a very nice boy who came over with a dustpan and broom and cleaned up after me. He even ran to get me a replacement pack. They acted like it was the fault of the store, but we all knew better. I'm glad I had my mask on. Maybe they won't recognize me next time I enter. I'll have to remember to wear a different mask.

We got to the cabin and added some more insulation to the well, then came inside and unpacked all those groceries. I was very careful with the blueberries, since there wasn't anybody with a broom and dustpan to help me there. I probably should've considered the storage space we have at the cabin. There is just enough space to handle supplies for a couple of days. So I put everything else on a bed. I figured if we did get bad weather and should lose power, we might be cold but we wouldn't be hungry.

On Christmas Eve I filled the tub with enough water for flushing, and 2 tea pitchers with enough water for brushing teeth (and set them on the back porch out of my way – there wasn't any more room on the bed). I made a huge pot of soup, and a large pan of roasted veggies, figuring Hubby could reheat our food outside on the grill if necessary, if he didn't freeze to death out there first. Then the rains came in. Sideways. It got heavier, the fog got thicker and the wind started howling. Around 7:00 that night I thought a hurricane was coming through. Then it was suddenly very quiet. You know how little kids get quiet after they have been noisy and you get suspicious? Hubby got suspicious. Sure enough, the loud rain had turned into quiet snow. And it was blowing sideways and covering the front door glass. It was a good time to watch *Rudolf the Red Nosed Reindeer*.

We had snow flurries all day on Christmas day, and the temperature dropped to 5°. Hubby worked on clearing the driveway with the tractor. He didn't have much success with that. In the afternoon he wanted me to get some exercise and walk with him down the driveway to see if our little one-lane road had been scraped. After putting on about 12 layers of clothes, I felt ready to go out. I think I have mentioned before that our driveway is long, steep and curved – not something you want to drive down in a sissy truck with sissy tires. It was fun walking in the snow. Wearing 12 layers makes single digit temperatures a little more bearable. I probably should have been more cautious, because I hit a slick spot. The next few minutes – probably just seconds – are all a blur. Let's just say I made it to the bottom of the driveway before Hubby did.

But the road had been cleared somewhat. The next morning we packed up to go, never having lost power. I went to the back porch to retrieve my 2 tea pitchers – both solid blocks of ice. Maybe the blueberry incident messed with my reasoning ability. Did I really expect to have fresh water sitting out there in 5° weather? Anyway, our sissy truck got us down the hill, mostly without incident with just a couple of slips here and there. How did you ever make it in Chicago?

HOTTEST NEW FASHION:
THE BRA HAT

Dear Jennifer,

Ellen's 40th birthday is in a couple of weeks. It's really hard to believe. In my mind she should still be 8. Bea is planning an all day celebration for her big sister. She wants to give Ellen 40 presents throughout the day and has been working on this project for several months. Naturally, she wants my assistance with this endeavor (and maybe a little help with financing, although she hasn't said anything yet).

The first few gifts will pertain to party stuff: balloons, banner, confetti, etc. Then gifts with an 80s theme start appearing: tee shirts that hang off the shoulder, tee shirt ties, leg warmers, hair scrunchies, you get the idea. The 80s weren't as bad as the 70s as far as fashion goes. I could show you some really horrible family photos of some of my guy relatives and friends wearing powder blue leisure suits …

Then Ellen will get a few pamper gifts, like bath salts, lotion and lip balm. I ordered a vintage 1981 Betty and Veronica comic book online. I am sure that in the days following her big birthday bash, Ellen will want to enjoy re-reading a Betty and Veronica comic while she is soaking her feet in Bea's bath salts. Hubby will deliver her lunch and a bunch of carnations at some point, probably around lunchtime, which would be so logical.

In the afternoon, Ellen will get a few gag gifts, one of which is the subject of this fascinating letter. When the girls were in their teens, we went shopping one day and entered the department store through the ladies' intimate section. Ellen saw a ginormous bra hanging on the rack. It could've been a watermelon container. For 2 watermelons. It required a heavy duty hanger. For each cup.

Ellen had a hard time wrapping her head around this, so she did what any normal person would do - she wrapped it around her head. She put one of the cups on her head, tied the straps under her chin, and said, in a very loud voice, "Who would need a bra this BIG?" Well, actually, the lady standing about 10 feet behind her did. She was waiting for her turn in the big girl section, but we seemed to be taking up all that space.

Bea and I could have stopped Ellen from making a big bra head out of herself, but sometimes you just have to let things happen in due course. Also, when you see the potential for some side-splitting laughter walking right through your door, it's just too tempting to keep your mouth shut and watch the scene unfold as you know it will. Ellen was mortified. She ducked down below the level of the big girl bra rack, waddled out of the intimates section, and came up for air over in Missy Sportswear. We hardly recognized her. By the time she popped up 50 yards away she was wearing a different shirt (complete with price tag and size strip), a pair of dark glasses, and a floppy straw hat – not a bra hat. Actually, Bea and I sort of hurried out of the intimates section ourselves, only we walked with our heads held high because we hadn't said anything embarrassingly funny that could be held over our heads for all eternity. As Bea and I were catching up to Ellen we turned to see the large lady who actually required a watermelon holder pick up the very bra Ellen had displayed on her head. Maybe she was looking at bras with a renewed interest. Maybe she was thinking outside the bra for a change.

We have teased Ellen about that scene for years, so naturally, we thought of giving Ellen her very own bra hat for her 40th birthday, just in case she might have forgotten about that other time. That would be practically impossible because during those rare times when the 3 of us get together, that bra story comes up. Let's do the math:

4 times a year we meet
x 25 years ago
= 100 times we have reminded her.

153

Not nearly enough reminders.

Back to the party plans. Bea bought the biggest bra they had at the thrift store - I didn't say all the gifts will be expensive – but it wasn't watermelon worthy. This cheap bra only rated honey dew melon status. Then I went to work. I cut the bra in half right between the cups, stacked the cups on top of each other, and tacked them together. Then I made a ruffle from some tulle I had stored in my 'extra tulle box' and sewed a few little flowers onto the side. It's fairly common knowledge that a plain bra hat ought to be simply and attractively adorned. This bra hat was actually quite charming. A fashion designer should always have a third party review her work for a fresh, honest perspective. I needed that third party and also a head model to check for size and placement of trims, so I called for backup: Hubby. He absolutely refused to be my model; in fact, he ran out of the house and locked himself in his workshop when I broached the subject. I had to try it on myself and I looked adorable in it. Since there was no one else around, I judged the bra hat to be the world's finest.

If I go commercial with a line of bra hats for the spring season, I might call my new product a brat.

Wait – I've got it: The Brass Ear. It just sings, doesn't it? Coco Chanel got her start making hats. I'll bet she never had a bra tucked away in her supply cabinet.

ICY DRIVEWAY

Dear Jennifer,

Last weekend Hubby and I went to the cabin to make another attempt at climbing Mt. Icicle. When we got there the driveway was almost a solid sheet of ice, but there were a few clear spots, which looked promising. Hubby tried to keep the truck tires on those as we fish-tailed up the drive. We stopped about a quarter of the way up, which was a lot farther than we got last year when we had snow trouble. You know I've had some near death experiences getting up that slippery slope.

We sat there in the driveway going through our options, which didn't take too long because there weren't many. But this year is a little different: we have a tractor. And we still had a little daylight left. Hubby decided to leave the truck there, then go get the tractor to ferry our stuff to the cabin. I sat in the truck while Hubby walked the rest of the way up. He checked the steep part going up to the cabin - much steeper and slicker than where the truck was stopped, and also the conditions around the barn – not quite as steep but just as slick. I sat in the truck playing Spider Solitaire. I can wait a long time if I'm safe inside a vehicle, my cell phone has full power, and I have Spider Solitaire handy.

I was there long enough for the daylight to go away completely and for the darkness take over. And it was getting pretty chilly in that unheated truck. Then I saw tractor headlights coming down the driveway. Our little dump cart was attached to it. I was a tad bit concerned about that tractor's inability to get stopped in time, but Hubby stopped the tractor right in front of the truck. Then he had to disconnect the dump cart so he could turn the tractor around to face the right way: uphill. There were some tense moments watching those big tractor tires slide all over the ice. Hubby finally got the tractor facing uphill after doing his famous 27-point turn. Then he reconnected the dump cart to the tractor and we put cooler, groceries, etc., into the dump cart.

Hubby drove the tractor all the way up to the cabin, pulling the little dump cart. Was there enough room for me in the dump cart? Oh, no. I got to walk uphill, in the snow, in the dark, and in the freezing cold. But last year taught me a lesson. Now I never go up there in cold weather without storing a spare pair of boots in the truck. A pair that fits *my* feet, not Hubby's. So I was prepared to trudge uphill in the snow. I also had the advantage of not having to carry supplies uphill. The little dump cart was taking care of that for me. So it wasn't so bad.

All in all, it took us 2 hours to get from here to the mountains and 1 hour to get up the driveway to the cabin. This is becoming a trend. The high Saturday was 34°. That certainly wasn't going to melt much ice. But Hubby had a plan: chop up the ice laying in the tire tracks and let the ice chips create traction. We went outside and down the driveway - no easy feat for clumsy feet. My footsteps didn't even break the top crust of snow. We hacked away at some ice in a few key areas and then Hubby left to try the truck. He backed down the hill a little to get a good start, and kept backing until he was out of sight. Or maybe he was sliding backwards and couldn't stop. I started getting nervous about my position in the driveway and walked up to a spot where the shoulder is wider and provides a safe dive down to the trail below, should I need a fast escape. I heard a mighty roar from our sissy truck and saw it doing the Electric Slide up the driveway at roughly 85 mph. The truck made it all the way to the barn and also managed to stop without denting anything important.

On Sunday Hubby tried moving the truck from the barn up the steep, icy driveway to the cabin. After watching his attempts, I am going to enter him in the next Winter Olympics Sissy Truck Figure Skating category. He slid all over the place and couldn't get up the hill. Really, I should have been playing *The Blue Danube* as he twisted and turned on the ice.

But Hubby had some creative ideas.
Plan A: lay little rows of gravel in front of the tires to drive up on
Plan B: use the winch

Plan C: let the truck sit there until April.

Fortunately, he didn't have to resort to B or C. I am so ready for spring and hoping the snow is over for this season and fully aware of how ridiculous that is, but really, these driveway adventures are getting a little tiresome.

ELLEN'S BIRTHDAY

Dear Jennifer,

The 'iced-over driveway at the cabin' saga is getting rather trite, so I won't bore you with the cold and dreary details. We didn't make it up the hill again, although it wasn't quite as bad as the other times. I had a special weapon in my ice and snow kit: a Cossack hat. My brother-in-law Fred gave Hubby this hideous hat 40 years ago as a Christmas gag gift and I kept it because, while it may be as ugly as homemade soap, it is quite warm. Killer, the chicken pit bull, barked nonstop when she saw me in that hat, so I had her insecurities to deal with, but I was cold at the time and that hat felt pretty good. It helped me trudge up the driveway without freezing my ears off and what more could a person ask of a Cossack hat than that? I refused to remove the hat, so Killer went back to her own home to sort through her feelings. Spring is just around the corner, which excites me beyond words.

But the big story this week is that Ellen's 40th birthday finally arrived. I'm very glad, because her little sister just about worked me to death prepping for this event. Bea had 40 presents (all numbered) - one of which was the bra hat, which went over big (DD big). She and 3-year-old Belle came to Ellen's house the night before and gave Ellen her first gift in advance: an envelope – marked with a big #1 of course – containing a gift certificate for free babysitting so that Jarrod could take Ellen to dinner that evening. Jarrod was in on this and was extremely helpful. While they were out, Bea got all the little kids to blow up balloons, make party favors, and decorate a large banner. Do you know how to make confetti poppers with Dixie cups? My grandchildren do. Poor Ellen had to do a little sweeping on her birthday. Bea also made her a delicious dirt cake, only it was an 'Older Than Dirt' cake. I knew it was delicious because when Hubby and I delivered gift #31 - lunch - all our little grandsweeties had Oreo smudges around their mouths.

Bea did a lot of research and loaded 80s music on her phone. She brought everyone a T-shirt that hung off one shoulder. I always thought they were a little slouchy looking, even when they were in style. All the females had to have their hair done up in an off-center ponytail, held in place by a scrunchie. Bea even found slap bracelets. Why do they still make those things? Oh, for 80s parties. I get it. Then they danced 80s dances to 80s music. The kids danced feverishly, probably because of the Older Than Dirt cake overindulgence, and I'm pretty sure they all slept soundly after that sugar high wore off.

I planned a strawberry layer cake as the *official* birthday cake. The Older Than Dirt cake was a 'just for fun' cake.

Rule #1 in baking: Don't try a new birthday cake recipe on an old person's birthday.
Rule #2: Follow the directions.

The cake layers turned out very nicely. Duncan Hines did not disappoint. I never said I was planning a cake from scratch. But the best part was supposed to be the strawberry cream cheese frosting. I was breaking Rule #1. It consisted of a block of cream cheese, a stick of butter and 3+ cups of powdered sugar. Into that I was supposed to mix in 1/4 cup of mashed fresh strawberries. In North Carolina fresh strawberries are not that great in February, so I bought sweet frozen strawberries and thawed them, breaking Rule #2. It smelled heavenly and licking the beaters was a delectable treat. But strawberry cream cheese soup was not the effect I was trying to achieve. I failed to account for the extra liquid in the frozen berries. Adding 3 more cups of sugar didn't change the consistency, although it did start to make me a little hyper. I have this rule about unlicked beaters.

Call mom! She will know what to do. She told me to serve slices of cake with the runny icing poured over each slice like a sauce. I knew she would have a good idea and her idea sounded delicious, but that would mean presenting a naked cake to Ellen while singing 'Happy Birthday', then slicing it for the sauce to go on. A naked cake for someone turning 40 simply did not appeal to me. I was really over stressing about this, especially since the grocery store is only 7 minutes away. Within a short 20-minute span I had fresh strawberries in my kitchen. When you're desperate, February strawberries aren't that bad.

The cake was wonderful. The best part was the strawberry cream cheese frosting, made according to directions. I sent the leftovers home with Ellen. It was her birthday, her cake, and her skinny little body. And also, I was a little full of all the extra frosting that didn't make it onto the cake. If you have never had strawberry cream cheese sauce, I highly recommend it.

IN THE OLD BARN

Dear Jennifer,

Last weekend we tried driving up the mountain driveway again with the same results as from the weekend before. Two inches of fresh snow sat atop the polar ice cap that covered the driveway and our truck simply refused to go up (note to self: If you're going to live on a mountain, invest in a four wheel drive vehicle). By this time we had a routine. I sat in the warm truck with the motor running while Hubby plodded uphill through the ice and snow to get the tractor. Hubby brought the tractor down, towing the little dump cart. This time I was offered a seat on the top of the plow. The plow is kept on the back of the tractor for balance. It kind of acts as leverage when Hubby is on a hill. The thought of why he needs leverage on a hill disturbs me, so I will move on from that topic.

The plow is old, solid and rusty. But it has a nice flat place across the top where two small rear ends can fit if necessary. My mom actually sits on the plow sometimes and Hubby takes her joy riding. She grew up on that property and I guess it makes her feel like a young girl again. Either that or she's getting a little bit dotty. So, after we loaded the cooler, laptop, a bag of groceries and my purse into the dump cart, I hoisted myself onto the plow. Really, sitting bare butt in the snow couldn't have been any colder than sitting on that plow. It had been parked in a 23° barn and a solid rusty metal plow is a perfect conductor of frigidity. As soon as Hubby slowed to negotiate a turn, I jumped off. It seemed warmer to climb up the hill in the snow and ice than to freeze my tail off. Showing up at the ER with a frostbitten tail just seemed like something I really didn't want to explain. Gives new meaning to the song *Blue Moon…*

So we snuggled in for the evening, drank hot chocolate and watched old *Perry Mason* episodes. Then Cousin Ambrose called. Would I like some of Granny Lola's old furniture? The cousins were cleaning out her farmhouse for a remodel and were getting rid of some things.

The only item of Granny's I had up to this point was a chipped cereal bowl. A relative gave it to me years ago and told me that Granny would want me to have it. Translation: I don't want it so I don't care if you take it. Oh, I did get 22 acres of mountain, but that's all. So I talked Hubby into taking me to Cousin Ambrose's the next morning. We slipped and slid down the driveway to the truck, which was still waiting for us down at the gate, and drove the half mile to Cousin Ambrose's barn. Papaw Herb built the barn back in the 40s and since then, the stairs to the loft have vanished. Cousin Ambrose gets up and down by leaning a step ladder, unopened, against the outside wall. That's fine for Cousin Ambrose, but he expected me to do the same thing. And I did, because as the oldest cousin, and future matriarch of the clan after Mom and Hecuba are gone, I must maintain an air of authority and strength. I didn't tell Cousin Ambrose that I'm afraid of heights. He already knew I'm as clumsy as an ox.

But I got up there with Hubby pushing my butt from the ground and Cousin Ambrose pulling my arms from the loft. Not something I would ever want to see posted on social media.

I chose the old 40s bookcase Granny used to put her little china figurines on. It looked like you might expect, but I needed it for grocery storage in the bedroom closet. You won't be surprised to learn that a thousand square foot cabin has very little storage space. I stow groceries in every nook and cranny - wherever there is a little room. Some people hoard toilet paper. I hoard canned goods and pancake syrup. You never know when you might get snowed in up there and can't get out for pancake syrup. And give me the kind with the high fructose corn syrup; I'm not interested in the healthy kind without all those good food additives.

Cousin Ambrose passed the bookcase down to Hubby and Hubby carried it to the truck. What about me? Poor Cousin Ambrose had to assist me out of the loft all alone. I hope his shoulder gets better soon.

We put the bookcase in the truck and drove 85 mph up the driveway, our plan being to get all the way to the top this time. But, no, that sissy truck stopped at its usual stopping point, and wasn't going any further. That truck seems to think it has its own private parking space on the driveway. Now…how to get that bookcase up the rest of the driveway to the cabin…? It was too wide for the little dump cart. Hubby hoisted it over his head and started plodding up the hill. What love. What sacrifice. I took back almost everything I had said about him last week.

After some heavy duty scrubbing with Amish Wood Milk, the bookcase looks as good as it ever did. It now sits in the closet and proudly displays cans of beans and tuna. And 2 bottles of pancake syrup. Everything is organized by category, of course. If any of the other cousins see my grocery case they are going to be so jealous. If that generous relative comes by for a visit, which is doubtful, I will put Granny's chipped cereal bowl on the bookcase as an accent piece.

LOW BATTERY

Dear Jennifer,

Last weekend at the cabin it was cold and windy outside and a good time to be cozy and warm inside. On Friday night I was snuggled in my warm bed in the loft, tucked into cuddly flannel sheets, with snow falling outside. So quiet and peaceful. It was like being in the middle of a Hallmark dream. How much cozier could it get?

CHIRP! Low battery!

What? Who said that? Someone has broken into our house and announced it!

CHIRP! Low battery!

It's a lady! She is inside the smoke detector! I clearly remember that the instructions on the smoke detector box said there would be a 'chirp' to announce a low battery. At 11:00 at night when you're snuggled in bed in the middle of a Hallmark dream with snow falling outside, it sounds more like a 'screech', not a chirp. And there was certainly no mention on the package of a lady invading our home announcing that the battery was low.

The only thing that kept me from having a heart attack right then and there was the strenuous effort I was making to avoid peeing on my cuddly flannel sheets. I didn't even know our smoke detector could speak. And she spoke and screeched every 2 minutes. And she wouldn't shut up. She was worse than the absolute worst mother-in-law. And she was several feet above the bedroom door. The step stool wasn't high enough for Hubby to reach and the ladder was in the barn. The barn is 300 feet from the cabin. I was determined NOT to walk down that dark, snowy hill at 11:00 at night to fetch a ladder in single digit temperatures. I certainly wasn't going to let Hubby go down there in the dark and cold all alone. So I strongly suggested that he use a bar stool.

Maybe Hubby didn't want to go get the ladder either because he made the bar stool work. He used the step stool to climb up to the bar stool and did a sort of gymnast balance beam maneuver to keep from falling off the bar stool as he removed the alarm from 11 feet above the floor. I am so glad he isn't afraid of heights. If I had been there all alone, I would have been forced to get the crowbar and either pry that alarm off the wall or beat it to death.

After Hubby replaced the batteries and I helped him carry a step stool and a bar stool back downstairs, I snuggled into my warm loft bed again and let my heart rate return to normal. That took about an hour and a half. There are no smoke alarm chirps or screeches in a Hallmark dream. Someone should be made aware of that.

COVID SHOT

Dear Jennifer,

My birthday was last week and I celebrated by getting my first Covid vaccine. Some people get gifts, some get cake, I got shot. To be honest, I got the gifts and the cake also, but the memorable part was going to the old mall and standing in line for an hour. The health department employee had informed me that the lines had been running smoothly and we should get there 15 minutes early. We got there 25 minutes early and stood behind hundreds of other old people. The line was not running smoothly. A young boy in an Army uniform (okay, all boys in uniform look young) gave us the preferred mask to wear (they didn't like the floral one my mom made for me) and told us where to stand. When you're in a large room with hundreds of other old people and can't take the mask off, it gets really hot really fast. And my mask had little prickly nylon threads that scratched my face the entire time. My mom-made specialty mask would have been so much more comfortable. So I was not having a fun birthday.

But the line did move along, although it was extremely annoying that the line didn't really build behind us. We were at the back of the line for the entire wait. So we could still have arrived on time and ended up in the same position. I would not have been so annoyed about that if those little nylon threads weren't tormenting my delicate skin. After getting their vaccinations, the hundreds of other old people were directed to a sitting area with timers that would go off after a 15-minute wait. I guess if your body is going to do something wacko after the shot, it only has 15 minutes in which to do so. I'm so glad I don't work there, because hearing that incessant beeping for the entire day would make me a little crazy. I'm betting those public health workers hear those beeps in their sleep. A thing like that can affect your REM.

So we got our shots, sat in our chairs, our timers were started, and then we just looked around at all the hundreds of other old people. Naturally, with all that free time on my hands, I compared myself to every other female in the room (I'm probably younger than her, and her, and her. I might be a little bit older than her but she is all stooped over, so I probably look a lot younger). You don't get it yet, but in another 30 years, you will. I would have done something more productive with my time like play Spider Solitaire on my cell phone, but Hubby kept up too much chatter for that to happen. Sometimes when he is in a room with hundreds of other old people, he starts rambling like an old geezer, which technically, he is.

Anyway, our beeper finally went off, we got our next appointment to come back in 3 weeks and we were out the door. Actually, I was pretty impressed with the whole assembly line thing. In Brent's county (a hillbilly hotbed where I have lots of kin) they announce that the vaccine will be available on a particular day at the old airstrip. No appointments or anything. Just first come, first served. So people are literally getting in line at 4:00 a.m. and sitting there in their cars until 10:00 a.m. to get the shot. And then when the medical people run out of shots they announce, "Well that's all for today folks!" and the remainder of the poor people who have been sitting there for hours leave dejected and unvaccinated. Aunt Hecuba lives there and I hope she made an appointment to get her shot at her doctor's office. I can't visualize her waiting in a line only to be told to go home. She would jump down from her SUV, hobble over to a healthcare worker, point her bony little finger in somebody's face and give them what for.

But I still got to celebrate a nice birthday. Bea's family came over at lunch time and brought food. Then Ellen's crew came over at dinnertime and brought food and birthday cake. Technically, it was Key Lime pie, not cake, but it was totally awesome and a slice of Key Lime pie can support a lit birthday candle.

I loved not cooking all day and for sure, not cleaning up. I think it would be absolutely wonderful to have a full time cook and housekeeper. If I ever win the lottery - really big lottery, not chump change lottery - I might consider buying a house with a maid's room off the kitchen and then putting a maid in it. Since I've never bought a lottery ticket and am too cheap to do so, the chance of my winning is even slimmer than that of those poor silly people who blow their meager paychecks on tickets every week. Maybe I could get extremely lucky and find a winning ticket like Charlie Bucket did in *Charlie and the Chocolate Factory*. Perhaps I should start looking down around curbs and gutters more often.

How did I get from Covid to gutters? I think one of the side effects of that shot is rambling on and on about useless and inane topics.

COVID REUNION

Dear Jennifer,

It was so nice to see you at work this week! I never thought seeing my coworkers at work would be weird, but having worked remotely for the last year has been weird, so just add that to the list.

I had to re-learn how to get ready to go to the office. First, there was the whole mascara thing. My tube had dried up, probably because the last time I used it was a year ago when we were sent home. Fortunately, there was a back-up tube, probably just as old as the other one, but at least it was still in the package from when I bought it a year ago. Then I had to remember how to stretch my mouth open just right and angle my face to heavily coat my eyelashes. They are virtually non-existent without 20-30 coats of mascara. Next I had to dig out earrings and re-pierce my ears when I put them on. I always figured that since my ears have been pierced for half a century, my earlobes should have a permanently solidified tunnel from front to back. They don't. Add a spritz of cologne. Oh, the sacrifices one must make for the sake of beauty.

I had to remind myself that pajama pants are totally unacceptable in the workplace, no matter how new, how clean, or how pretty they are. Thankfully, my jeans still fit. And I found a clean shirt that didn't have food stains on it. And no fuzzy socks, either. I had to wear the trouser socks with flats. I felt like I was going to a formal wedding.

But then there was the drive to town. I had forgotten how evil those drivers are on the main road and in the year I have been home, I have lost all my aggressive driving skills. It took me years to perfect them – tailgating, switching in and out of lanes, cutting off the other drivers. Now I drive like a wimpy old lady.

I had to reprimand myself for making fun of my mom who

schedules all her errands between 10:00 and 2:00, avoiding school bus traffic, tractor trailer traffic and rush hour traffic. When she was employed she drove on the interstate into downtown, and then parked in a huge parking garage. I thought she was a very brave woman. Now that she is retired, she drives like a wimpy old lady. Aunt Hecuba is the oldest aggressive driver I know. She is absolutely fearless when she is behind the wheel, not like the nervous passengers in her car. And she is not afraid to push the gas pedal a little to get to where she is going. She ranks near the top of my most admired drivers list. Thankfully, there are several relatives in her county who are law enforcement officers, so they can sort of keep an eye on her and give her plenty of space when she needs to get to the mall.

Off on a tangent again. And then we were in the office. I had to sit in my seat. I couldn't run downstairs and throw a load of clothes in the washer. I couldn't run to my secret stash of truffles, milk chocolate miniatures, and dark chocolate bars with sea salt caramel filling. I couldn't look out the window to see what the Amazon truck brought the neighbors across the street. And I had to wear that mask for three hours. My nose itched. My glasses fogged. The straps gave me Dopey ears. I've become much too comfortable at home. Fortunately, we are only required to be at the office a few days this month, and then back to our new 'normal' – working from home.

And then I had to drive home. It was the morning trip all over again, only backwards. When I got home I called my mom and talked nice to her as a way to make up for all those times I've made fun of her wimpy old lady driving – not that she ever knew I had done that. Only an idiot, or a very brave person, or someone with a death wish, would make fun of my mom's driving to her face. Then I called my Zuzu, my comrade. "I'm a wimpy old lady now." My sister and *former* comrade replied, "The whole family has talked about nothing else for the last two years."

THE GREAT TRAIN RIDE

Dear Jennifer,

Several weeks ago my mom was chatting with Bea when the subject of travel came up. I'm not sure why that subject would come up because my mom doesn't travel. She has left the state 2 times in her entire lifetime and never saw the ocean until she was in her 40s. Anyway, she casually mentioned to Bea that she had always wanted to ride on a train. She has visited Tweetsie Railroad, but that hardly counts.

Bea called me a few days later with her brilliant idea. I would take Bea and her grandmama to the train station in High Point, race the train back to Greensboro, pick them up and take the 3 of us to lunch. I agreed to the plan and then Hubby heard about it. He wanted to go. Then Ellen heard the plan and she wanted to go. You can see where this is headed. Within hours, the whole plan had changed and 13 of us were going, including me, because since it had turned into a family event, it wouldn't be the same without me. Naturally.

Then Ellen said that by the time we got to Greensboro, we would just be starting to enjoy the ride. The next stop on the line was Burlington, so Bea started planning that. Finally everything was in place; the tickets were purchased and we all started looking forward to our exotic trip to Burlington.

Last Thursday was the big day and Ellen and Jarrod were sick. Grandmama and I picked up Athena, Hawkins and Julius, because how can you deny little kids an exciting train ride after it has been promised? Ellen read them the riot act for about 45 minutes. They were practically perfect the entire day.

When the train finally arrived at the High Point station, its choo choo noise was drowned out by kids screaming. But the train employees were nice to us anyway. We found our seats and I was glad we decided to stretch the trip to Burlington, because no one was anywhere close to settling down by the time we hit Greensboro. The ride to Burlington was very relaxing for us - very noisy for the other passengers. I hope none of them were looking forward to a quiet, peaceful trip.

We arrived in Burlington and walked to a little shopping center nearby. Bea had already checked out the local eateries, so there would be no surprises. We found a hot dog diner and moved in like an army. With a crowd our size, maintaining a 6-foot distance was hardly an option. But the 2 construction workers sitting at the largest table in the diner got up and gave us their seats. Very kind men. Or very afraid of noisy children. Maybe the latter, because they ran out of the diner without finishing their meals.

The diner seemed to clear out right after our crowd entered. Maybe they were just finished eating. Maybe they were overwhelmed to be in the presence of such overjoyed, hyper, rambunctious, talkative children. Rambunctious children who kept the restrooms busy for most of our stay. And had to go back again after we had left the building. Very patient diner employees. Hubby left a most generous tip.

Grandmama was having a ball.

We headed to the park. Hubby took a big person and half the little people to an ice cream parlor while the rest of us waited our turn. I'm not sure how little kids can consume an entire hot dog, fries and a big drink, and then want the largest cone on the display case. But they can. Then it was time for the other half of our group to go. We needed to make the time stretch because we had a couple of hours to wait before our return trip. There was a nice park nearby and we sat there enjoying our ice cream and the scenery. Oddly, we had the park all to ourselves. And those kids consumed every bite of their ice cream. Where did they manage to put it?

Then I remembered what I miss about having little kids. It went something like this:
I'm going to the bathroom - why don't you go with me?
No.

Sure?

No. Don't want to.

Okay, then you wait here with our group and I'll be right back.

5 minutes later … Mimi, I have to go.

Of course you do. Let's find a bathroom in a store somewhere that's not as convenient as the one I offered to take you to just 5 minutes ago.

Then it was time to walk back to the depot. Our group was making quite an impression on the railroad employees. We must've overstayed our welcome. When the train pulled in and we headed for the car, the depot employee told the conductor to put us in our OWN car. He looked at us and smiled and said they had heard about us and had a special car just for us. The kiddos were feeling pretty special, but I know how to read between the lines. I also checked to be sure that the 'special' car was connected to the rest of the train.

It was a very short day, but the kiddos asked if we could please make this a yearly event. Yes, but only if your mother comes with us next year. I was stiff and sore for 3 days.

FIGHTING OFF KILLER

Dear Jennifer,

Mom went with us to the cabin last weekend. She loves to putter in the flower beds at her house so I gave her a flower bed of her very own in the mountains. It's the only way to get her to come and visit us. But on Saturday we couldn't do any yard work because Auntie Hecuba was coming over at 10:30 and Mom didn't want to be dirty when Auntie got there. I guess you never get too old to look nice for your big sister, although, in this case, Auntie is anything but a big sister. Her weight and age are the same - 90.

Hubby dropped us off at Granny Lola's old farmhouse where Auntie was waiting. They had an appointment with Cousin Ambrose to go through the old barn and see all the old stuff he had pulled out of the farmhouse over the years.

First we went into the old house. Killer, the chicken pit bull, heard us and did her ferocious barking routine until I told her it was just us. When she recognized me, her bark changed into a 'let me in and play' whine. I told her to wait outside and we would be along shortly. As soon as we stepped outside Killer was all over us. Literally. She nipped at heels. She jumped up on us. She had been in the creek - ghastly. The clean shirt I was wearing just to impress Auntie was already smelling like wet dog. And we hadn't even crossed the road to Ambrose's barn yet.

Suddenly Killer ran toward Mom and jumped her from behind. Auntie screamed and I just stopped breathing. Killer is a chicken pit bull, but she isn't a *little* chicken pit bull. Fortunately, Mom didn't fall. But it scared Auntie because that is exactly what happened to her 25 years before when the family dogs were playing, knocked her down and broke all her leg bones. Not really – it was actually just a couple of knees. But it took her a long time to recover and she still walks with a cane. This experience gave her some serious flashbacks. So I told the sisters to go through Ambrose's barn and have a good time, and I would hold onto Killer. As you may recall, I visited that barn earlier this year and had to ease myself out of the loft onto a rickety step ladder. I really didn't feel the need to go back again.

The sisters took their own sweet time looking around (and NOT going up the ladder). Where was Ambrose? In the meantime, I had to find Killer's favorite scratching place. This was not fun, especially since I had to hold onto her collar the entire time. And she was still wet with creek water. My fingernails will never feel clean again. Every once in a while she would get really frisky, jump all over me, and I would have to wrestle her back down to the ground. I was really wishing for a stick to throw so we could release some of that energy, but the only stick close by was Hecuba. She was having fun looking at old stuff while I was rolling around in the grass playing championship wrestling with an excited wet dog. Killer was loving it, and well she should. She had the use of all 4 limbs as we rolled and tumbled. I only had 3 limbs to fight her off. Number 4 was being used to hold onto her collar so she wouldn't run over to play with the sisters.

Finally the sisters were finished and they started walking our way. I promised to hold Killer until they were safe in the car. As you might expect, an 88-year-old and a 90-year-old are in no hurry to get to the car, no matter how much their daughter/niece is rolling around on the ground in a dogfight. 4 hours later their car doors were securely shut and I let go of Killer's collar. She was so excited. Now she could jump on me some more and bite my heels during that long walk to the car. I wanted to give her a good swift kick, but I don't have that many friends and I need to keep the few friends I do have. It's a wonder I was allowed in Auntie's nice car. I was covered in muddy paw prints, dog spit and loose grass. They didn't seem to notice my stains or smell at the time. They were so busy talking about sister things, I'm not even sure they noticed *me*.

That night I dreamed of a pack of wet dogs who were stalking me and one of them had his teeth locked onto my rear end. I couldn't walk without dragging him along, making it feel like I was walking with 6 legs. It was quite difficult to walk that way in my dream. I finally managed to free myself when I got to the car, climbed inside, and closed the door. Now I know what to do if Killer, the chicken pit bull, ever locks her teeth onto my rear end – find a car and get in.

KUDZU FIGHTING

Dear Jennifer,

It's that time of year when Hubby and I go kudzu fighting. Actually, at this time of year we go kudzu *hunting*.

And we were not disappointed. Fortunately, the kudzu is limited to roughly three acres on the steep side of the hill. Unfortunately, the kudzu is limited to roughly three acres on the *steep* side of the hill. Carrying our tools while slipping down the slopes makes us exhausted before we even get started. So the engineer had a plan. This plan required leaving me unattended while he fetched more supplies. Killer, the chicken pit bull, was there to keep me company. Thank goodness she wasn't in play mode or I would still be pulling sticks and dead leaves out of my hair.

Hubby returned with a mile length of very sturdy rope. I'll never know where he gets all these supplies. He anchored one end to the golf cart. Poor little golf cart. It was probably missing a beautiful golf course and escorting a couple of really cool people around with two golf bags in its bag well. Instead it was chugging along our little trail in the woods escorting two old geezers with a pick axe, chain saw and shovel in its bag well. And now it had to anchor a mile long rope to pull those two old geezers back up the hill.

Anyway, Hubby anchored one end of the rope securely to the golf cart and tied the other end around his waist. Then, acting like a beginner rappelling student, he came down to meet me quickly and safely. He simply isn't happy if he isn't inventing a new and improved method of doing a simple job. So he reached my spot and saw several fresh kudzu vines leaning over the road. Attacking the kudzu from the road would seem safer, but as our place is on a curved, one-lane road and the locals drive like they are from Daytona, working from the road really isn't a good option. Since he was secure and safe, the only thing working against us was that we still had a half mile of unused rope. I had to pull the excess and wrap it around a few trees so that Hubby could lean over the steep part and start whacking away. The steep part is probably at a 90° angle to the road, but he would only fall about ten feet if I were to let go of my end.

And I did consider it, but only for a second. Who would go kudzu fighting with me if Hubby were in a body cast? And what if he remembered what happened after recovering from his brain injuries? I didn't want to spend the rest of my life looking over my shoulder. So I did my part to keep him safe. Then it was my turn. I simply was not going to wear that rope around my waist. I could just picture myself losing my footing and swinging from an oak tree like a big flabby pendulum. So I just wrapped one arm around the rope and held on while I attacked kudzu with the other arm. I was literally at the end of my rope. And I have yet to mention that the poison ivy looks really healthy this year - probably because we have almost eradicated the kudzu and have given the poison ivy more growing space. Also, the barbed wire fencing is still lying in the same place it has been for 90 years, but it is so rusty and hides among the dead leaves so well, I always forget it's there.

We spent about an hour seeking and destroying kudzu until I closed my eyes and told Hubby I couldn't see any more of it. I was whipped. But the beauty of the rope idea was about to be revealed to me. In my exhausted state I didn't have to climb back up that steep hill on my own. I had my trusty rope to pull up on. Hubby offered to start driving the golf cart - slowly - and pull me up the hill. I did have some pride left so I declined. Again, I envisioned myself losing my footing and getting dragged up the hill, gathering dead leaves, sticks and poison ivy between my teeth, or being yanked over rocks and between trees like a fat little cartoon character.

Next week's note might be a whiny tale of my poison ivy suffering.

SASQUATCH RESCUE

Dear Jennifer,

While I was struggling with Killer, the chicken pit bull, and getting covered in dog spit the other day and the sisters were perusing Ambrose's barn, Mom thought she caught a glimpse of Granny Lola's old kitchen table in the loft. I was interested, not because the table was pretty - far from it. It was so ugly, Granny always kept a tablecloth on it. But I was interested anyway.

So I called Ambrose and asked if I could go shopping in his loft. Obviously, I was really interested in this ugly table because you will probably remember how I have to get up to the loft. Ambrose has not improved access to the barn since my last visit. So Hubby drove me over and Killer, the wet hyper chicken pit bull, was there to greet us. I was so not interested in dog wrestling that day. Sasquatch and his daughter Sassy Squatch were there. Sassy had been to a tea party and was wearing a dress with a sequined bodice and tulle skirt. She was so cute. Killer thought so too, and jumped all over Sassy. That dress will never see another tea party again. Actually, I see a can of Lemon Pledge in its future as a rag bag item.

Anyway, Ambrose kept Killer off me as I headed toward my favorite rickety step ladder leaning against the barn. Ambrose scrambled right up into the loft. He must spend a lot of time up there. The menfolk and I have developed a routine - Ambrose pulls both my arms from the loft and usually Hubby pushes my rear end from his position on the ground. But now we had additional manpower. Sasquatch gave my tail one push and I practically flew up into the loft. If I had had any pride before, I certainly didn't have any by this time.

The old table was up there, resting on 2 planks. I really wanted to see it on the ground because standing in a rickety loft on a couple of rickety planks is not fun when you have a fear of heights. Suddenly a previously unnoticed cat jumped down on one of the planks and I think I lost one of my lives. I didn't even know Ambrose had a cat.

So Ambrose passed the table out of the loft to the two men not stupid enough to climb the step ladder. Then it was my turn to exit the loft. I had been through this before. I probably would have made it to the ground safely if I hadn't had all that attention. Sasquatch told me not to worry - he would catch me. I certainly didn't want Hubby catching me. He is old and breakable and we chose the cheaper accidental insurance option through Blue Cross.

Anyway, I started down the ladder and almost made it. But I just don't perform well with a large audience. I completely missed the last two rungs and stepped off into thin air. Hubby stepped out of the way so that Sasquatch could keep his promise. Also I think Hubby was afraid it would kill him if I landed wrong. I'm not as lightweight as I used to be. Sasquatch did catch me around my middle and there I was, dangling 2 feet off the ground in the arms of a huge teddy bear. To be honest, he only used one arm.

He knew that I've been sharing his exploits with you, so he was probably just giving me more subject matter for the Chronicles of Sasquatch. I sure hope he doesn't tell this to his huntin' buddies. So humiliating.

But the good news is that the ugly table is now mine. It is stained, cracked and not plumb, but it's made with broad boards and wooden pegs and it started out with Granny Lola and Papaw Herb back in 1928. After a loving treatment of Amish wood milk it doesn't look a bit better. And I'm throwing a tablecloth over it and using it just like Granny did, hoping one of my grandchildren loves it enough someday to use it and tell his/her children the risks Mimi took to get that table: how she was rescued from a two-foot fall by the legendary Sasquatch.

HOUSEWORK

Dear Jennifer,

Last weekend we had to get ready for overnight guests. Pru, an old friend of mine, is planning a trip to the cabin this week and that trip includes her mother-in-law, Emmaline. I know Emmaline and she is a very neat and tidy person. Everything I am not. Housework and I never got along. Call me lazy – it doesn't even bother me. My lack of housekeeping skills is well-known. It was actually made into a skit at church once. It was very funny and I laughed along with everybody else in our large congregation. We ALL knew I have had a brand new iron since 1973. And it still works great, or so I assume. I really wouldn't know.

But I had to really, seriously, thoroughly clean the cabin. Hubby vacuumed for me. He is such a sweetie – kudzu killer and vacuum man. I swept all the hardwood floors, plus the porches. The places under furniture that were unreachable by broom got hit with the dust mop. I actually dusted lamp shades, and all the furniture. I scrubbed countertops, and the bath fixtures. I vacuumed the mattresses. Why? Because Emmaline might bring her magnifying glass, that's why. Naturally, I changed all the sheets. I actually do that on a regular basis. Changing sheets and unloading the dishwasher are the 2 housekeeping chores I faithfully perform, mainly because I like to sleep and eat on clean surfaces. Even lazy slobs have standards. And sheets and dishwasher are the limit of my standards. I even got the crumbs out of the silverware tray. And that's another one of life's mysteries. How DO crumbs end up in my silverware tray? No one in my family eats over the silverware tray. I make them use plates like regular people.

I was feeling pretty good about myself. Heaven forbid that Emmaline should find out that I don't even know where my own vacuum cleaner is stored here in town. Maybe it's with the Christmas stuff. That would be a logical place, since the once-a-year items would be all together.

Just after Pru married into this family, Emmaline mentioned to me that she is insecure around me. Me? I gave her my best blank stare. I just had to know what it was that I do that could possibly make anyone on the planet insecure. I do avoid work better than anyone I know, but somehow, this doesn't seem to be a quality that would intimidate someone. In fact, I do so little, I always assumed that everyone associated with me felt extremely *secure*. I can't even remember now what superlative qualities she seemed to think I had, but I do remember thinking that Pru must have laid the praise on a little thick when she was singing my praises to Emmaline. Perhaps Pru doesn't really care for her mother-in-law and was just making nice things up about me to annoy her. I got Pru a little present for building me up and making me look good. I think I hid it behind the vacuum cleaner. Maybe Hubby will find it for me.

Which reminds me - I just realized that I forgot to dust the ceiling fans at the cabin. Emmaline is up there right now lying between clean sheets under a dusty ceiling fan in an antiseptic cabin. She is probably feeling a lot more secure right now.

A LITTLE SQUIRRELY

Dear Jennifer,

Time for another story from the Family Vault of Mostly True Tales …

Hubby, Ellen and I came home one afternoon and noticed some things slightly awry. The fireplace screen was lying on the floor. Not a good sign. The special peach I was saving just for me until it ripened to perfection was lying on the kitchen floor with a bite out of it. I distinctly remembered NOT leaving it on the floor when we left earlier in the day. And I certainly hadn't taken a bite out of it because it hadn't ripened to perfection yet. Also, the teeth marks looked more squirrely than girly. Another bad sign. We knew we had a visitor in the house. But where was it? Ellen was five years old and terrified. Bea was expected in another two months and didn't care.

We followed debris and destruction from room to room. There was squirrel poop on every single flat surface in every single room. He pooped on windowsills, planters, end tables, even the piano. He must've spent the entire day in there. After he had struggled to scratch the flue open to get out of the fireplace. Then we got to the living room. My tall houseplants looked like damaged trees after a hurricane. They were probably as close to a tree as our guest could find. He also discovered the windows. Those little squirrel teeth had gnawed all the way through the wood between the window panes and stopped only when they reached the caulk, or whatever that stuff is that goes between window panes.

We were running out of rooms, but we were certainly not running out of poopy trails. He was pretty easy to follow. Ellen's room was at the end of the house and that's where we found our home wrecker. Squirrels look a lot bigger when they are inside your house. He had knocked the curtains off one window and was hiding behind what was left of a curtain at the other window. Actually, the front part of him was hiding. His big rear end and fluffy tail were in plain sight. I assume that his thoughts went something like "I can't see them, so they can't see me". We quietly closed the door and called Animal Control. All the while, Ellen was insisting that we get that animal out of her room. How do you reason with a child over something like this? For that matter, who is going to explain it to me?

A short, wiry little guy appeared at our door with a big net, ready for action. No problem, he assured us that he had done this many times, so we shut him in Ellen's room with the Tiny Beast. Based on the bumps, thumps, whacks and smacks we heard coming out of there, he may have done this many times, but he hadn't done it *enough* times. Hubby had to go in and assist, which was a good thing, because the short, wiry little guy was gasping for air and looked to be near death's door.

Hubby opened a window, pushed out the screen, and together the two humans scared the nasty squirrel toward the window where he escaped. I'm pretty sure the squirrel was as happy to be out of there as we were to see his tail go over the side. I think the short, wiry little guy did more damage than the squirrel. A mattress was off the bed. Blankets were everywhere. Why? Who knows? He was left unattended. The canopy on Ellen's bed was askew. This kid wanted her room fixed. Right then. And there was more squirrel poop in her room than all the other rooms combined. I think we can blame that one on stress.

It only took a few days to clean up and straighten everything (and take broken houseplants out to the woodpile) but that house never felt sanitary again. Ellen still hates squirrels. I'm still thinking about that peach.

FOUR TUBING GENERATIONS

Dear Jennifer,

Every summer our family gets together at the cabin to celebrate summer birthdays and if the weather cooperates we try to go tubing together. This time I asked my 88-year-old mom if she would like to join us. She grew up beside the river but in those days her family was busy farming and there was no time for recreation. The river served as a drinking fountain for the cows and that was about all. Mom never learned to swim and I expected her to turn me down. To my surprise, she said she would like to go.

The girls and their families arrived Saturday morning. The kids all lined up for sunscreen spray, so Hubby got in the back of the line for his turn. He has always been our biggest kid. Ellen kept spraying and didn't even notice the extra kid. The nicer rafts had coolers, so all the kids, Hubby included, thought we needed to make use of them. We had to spend some time filling the coolers with snacks and soft drinks.

My mom came outside dressed and ready to go. She was wearing a hat, long sleeve shirt, capris, and tennis shoes with socks. She was probably wearing underwear also, but I was afraid to ask. Mom has always been very attractive and wants to stay that way so she didn't want age spots popping up while she was out in the sun. I guess she failed to notice that the rest of us looked pretty rough indeed. Too bad the Guinness people weren't there to record a new category for:

Most Clothes Worn At One Time to Get Wet

Hubby did award her with the title:

Oldest Person Ever to Go Tubing on the New River

She didn't appreciate his sense of humor, especially when he compared her age to just a little younger than the river. We

185

were terribly proud of her for participating with us, so a little teasing was called for. Several folks on the river praised my mom for getting out there and having fun. She was pretty popular that day.

Some highlights of our trip:
A family having a picnic high on the bank over the river was waving to tubers and kayakers as we passed. We thought they were terribly friendly. We didn't realize that their little kids had a fake snake hanging from a tree branch. The naughty little kids would lower this snake via fishing line down on unsuspecting tubers and kayakers. Poor Jarrod. Good thing his lower half was in the water - the river got a little warmer when the snake tapped Jarrod on the shoulder. If the snake had tapped my mom's shoulder I would have been torn between performing CPR on my mom and thrashing a little kid's setter.

The river was so low we often got hung up on rocks. It didn't bother my mom even a little bit since she just sat there relaxing and taking it all in while one of us gave her a tow. At one point, Ellen was so busy moving tubes away from rocks that we all floated away from her and she had to walk for a while. She lost her crocs in the current twice.

The current often turned us around so that we were facing backwards. Mom didn't like that at all so I used my foot as an oar to turn us around. Let's just say I was walking funny the next day. I didn't even know I had muscles there.

Belle thought I was her personal butler and asked me for a snack about 4 times. She has a real thing for snacks in a tubing situation. I don't think she appreciated the fact that I was busy turning her great-grandmother around to face the right direction.

And then Mom called Aunt Hecuba and told her all about her trip up the river. Now Auntie wants to go. Auntie is 91 years old now, weighs as much as 2 king-sized pillows, walks with a cane, and totters on uneven terrain. I am certainly not willing to break my aunt so that she can even things up with her baby sister. Just imagining getting her into and out of the river gives me chills. Can you picture me staggering across slippery river rocks with Hecuba in my arms and NOT falling? Me neither. Cousin Junior wouldn't like me anymore. And mom is asking when we are going again. Heavy sigh.

SENIOR

Dear Jennifer,

Eloise, my friend and neighbor, and Certified Fraud Examiner, does our taxes every year and refuses to accept payment for it. That's one of the reasons why she is my friend (she also makes delicious chicken salad for me). She had a birthday recently so while I was at the grocery store last week I picked up a gift card for her. When it was time to check out, the cashier wanted to know how much to put on it. I told her to put $100 on it, not because I am so generous to all my friends, but to pay Eloise for doing our taxes. It's the only way she will accept payment. And it still isn't enough for what she does. (Well, except for the fact that Eloise knows all my business. Fortunately, she keeps secrets. It would help, though, if I had a few secrets on her – just to keep things fair and balanced). Technically, I owe her some more money. You just can't get a good tax accountant for $100. Okay, I can, but to be fair, I should give her some more birthday money.

Things were going fine at the checkout. My watermelon rolled along on its own down to the register. I wish I hadn't bought it. It only rated a C- on my watermelon scale. Not nearly sweet enough. Why don't they give classes on how to pick a good watermelon? I hate guessing and getting it wrong, which is what I have done all summer with watermelon.

And then a nice store manager approached me. "Ma'am, is this card for you?"
[Well…duh.]
Manager: "Is it for you, or maybe a gift for someone you know?"

What is this? Do we have to be specific now when we buy gift cards at a grocery store? So I had to explain that I was indeed buying this gift card as a gift for someone I know whose name is Eloise and she is my friend and has been for many years and I want to remain friends with her because I like her and because she does my taxes every year for free, which is another reason I like her.

Manager: "Sorry to sound so mean, but scammers are swindling seniors out of their money by sending them to the store to buy gift cards and then giving the scammers the activation codes. We are just trying to look after our seniors."

Seniors? She actually called me a senior out loud? In front of an entire store full of people? I know how old I am and I know I qualify as a senior, and have for several years; however, we just don't come right out and announce it like that. I'm a little pudgy too, but there's no reason to advertise it ("Ma'am, are those doughnuts for you, or are you possibly buying them for someone you know? We are just trying to look after our little pudgy customers"). Let me just say that she was no spring chicken, either.

Maybe it was my long grey hair flying all over my head. I missed my May haircut appointment with Lana Nichols and she can't see me until July, so I do look a little wild and woolly. Maybe the whole incident was because of the store's location. This particular grocery store is down the hill from the rest home. The store manager probably thought I was an escapee having a lark before they caught me and escorted me back up the hill. At this point I should add that a fast food burger joint gave me the senior discount many years before my senior status was legal and binding, and Hubby still brings this up at family gatherings.

On the evening of Eloise's birthday, Hubby and I went over with the gift card that wasn't nearly as much fun as it had started out to be. When we told Eloise and her husband Theodore about the emotional suffering I endured to get her this gift, Theodore said, "They not only called you a senior; they called you a *stupid* senior."

RANDOM THOUGHTS

Dear Jennifer,

This week's letter is just some random thoughts because none of them was interesting enough to expand to a full letter-size piece of paper. I can only embellish so much.

I've had a cold for about two weeks and I was 99% sure it was a cold because I've been getting colds for decades and they always act the same. Nevertheless, when I went in for my annual physical, my doctor wanted to be sure. I had to go through the secret entrance (I know it was a secret entrance because there was no one sitting at the door wanting a co-pay. It was like being Batman and driving through that awesome cave entrance he used to have). And before I knew what was happening, a ramrod was shoved up my nose. I couldn't cry because this large projectile went all the way up to my eye and clogged my tear duct. Then the nurse did the same thing in my other nostril. I hope I didn't hurt her when I kicked her. She is a really sweet little girl when she isn't being abusive. I've never felt so violated. I think she created a third nostril up there. I breathed funny for five days. I only had to wait ten minutes for the results. It was a cold. I sure hope I don't get a bill for that.

And remember when we took my mom tubing on the river a few weeks ago? I got a little sunburn but not a painful one. I forgot all about it until I scratched my leg Sunday and started peeling the bottle tan right off my legs. They were as flaky as river birch bark. Hideous. So I had to smooth things out. Now the flakes are all gone, but my tan is missing in key places. My legs look like Grandpa Daniel's brown and white Guernsey cows. Somewhat attractive on a cow. Not so pretty on skinny white legs.

A transitional phrase should go here but I can't think of one, so I can't segue properly into my next topic.

Which is: How is your daughter adjusting to college life? Does she have a nice roommate? Has she gotten homesick? Does she like her classes? How are YOU adjusting to empty nesting?

I remember taking Ellen to App State. I cried solid from Boone to North Wilkesboro. After that I had what my mom calls 'the snubs' the rest of the way home. Then when we got home I found a sweet letter Ellen had left for me and I cried another two days.

When it was time to take Bea to App State I cried solid from Boone to North Wilkesboro. Then when we got home I found a sweet letter she had left for me and cried another 15 minutes. And then it dawned on me that I had a new room to turn into my own. Bea's old bedroom became my craft room. And now it's my craft room, office and gym. It has been great for crafts. I can leave my supplies all over the place and close the door to nosy people who want to see what sort of housekeeper I am. Actually, no one has ever done that, but if they did, I could close the door. And the sort of housekeeper I am is really no secret.

It has been a great office for working remotely. I don't have to put all my stuff on a dining room table like some of our coworkers have to do. I have a nice view – I know when the mailman has stopped by, and when the guy next door walks his dog – and I have a door. It would be very hard to come back to the office without my view and my door.

And I have a gym there as well. Okay, it's only a treadmill. I hang clothes on it. But I could use it as a treadmill if I wanted to. I just don't want to.

Anyway, when your daughter comes home, she will hug you and tell you what a wonderful mother you are and offer to help out in the kitchen and tell you she never knew she had it so well at home. And you will be glad you didn't put her up for adoption when she turned 13.

GIRLS DAY

Dear Jennifer,

We celebrated our annual Girls Day a couple of weeks ago. It has been a tradition with us for about 20 years. Part of the tradition is telling Hubby he can't go. But that doesn't stop him from asking every year. He finally got smart and started declaring Daddy Daughter Day (he calls it D^3 because he is so mathematically witty).

The first Girls Day was just Ellen, Bea and me going to a fancy mall. I think it was in Durham. It was wherever my first Cheesecake Factory experience was. I made a mental note to split a meal 3 ways next visit so that I could enjoy ALL of my dessert. As I recall, the next year we did exactly that, but I still had too much to eat and had to get my dessert to go. I seriously was not going to leave the Cheesecake Factory without a piece of cheesecake. Through the years our Girls Day plans have taken us different places and we have experienced some fun activities. We have painted pottery, shopped for antiques and books, taken tours of beautiful homes, and shopped some more. Lunch is a given.

But this year another generation joined us, raising our total number of girls to 5. We got a little fancy by planning a weekend trip to the cabin. No Boys Allowed. We made 8 days' worth of plans and tried to cram in as much fun as we could into our 3 days. But first we had to eat. We went all out since it was Girls Day and ate at the Hillbilly Grill – not on the same level as the Cheesecake Factory. Probably not even on the same planet as the Cheesecake Factory. It might come as no surprise to you to learn that we fit right in there with the other hillbillies. The owners and wait staff were all family – not a big deal in our little mountain town – and so nice to us. They made us feel right at home there. Anyway, the food was great and all 5 of us enjoyed fries made 5 different ways, so there was a lot of passing and trading back and forth.

The next big Girls Day item on our schedule was shopping. On D^3 the girls get to shop for clothes which Dad finances. But on Girls Day we shop for fun stuff. We went to a vintage and antique shop and had a ball touching and sneezing over lots of rusty and dusty items. There was nothing in there that any of us needed. Who needs an old rusty watering can with a round bottom? Actually, Ellen thinks she does and I sneaked back later and bought it for her for Christmas. I left the ugly, ornate Victorian cast iron mailbox where it was, mainly because it was too heavy to pick up.

By this time we were exhausted so we finally went to the cabin and immediately jumped into our pajamas. Bea started unpacking groceries and getting organized, or so I thought. Ellen wanted an up close view of the barn quilt I had painted, and we walked down to the barn so I could get bragged on a little. She loved it and went on and on about the gorgeous design and colors I had chosen (I had to admit to her that the computer had chosen those gorgeous colors).

When we got back to the cabin, there was a surprise birthday party waiting for me. Bea had been busy blowing up balloons and setting out birthday cake while Ellen was distracting me down at the barn. My birthday was 6 months ago so it was a REAL surprise. Then I realized Ellen was just toying with me to get me out of the house so that Bea could setup. Ellen had seemed very impressed with the lovely barn quilt, but I realized by then it was only a ploy. Now I will never really know if my barn quilt is as exquisite as she said it was or if it is only just plain beautiful.

Girl movies for 3 days, including *Pride and Prejudice* with Keira Knightley (that's our favorite and we have seen ALL the versions), pedicures and lots of chocolate and hot tea.

And then Cousin Junior checked in on us. He knew we were up there alone, so he wanted to be sure we were fine. There we were in our daytime pajamas, because No Boys Allowed. Fortunately, Cousin Junior has known me all his life so his expectations weren't very high.

The highlight of our adventure was getting 2 clear nights to watch the Perseid meteor showers. It is a rare August night when there are no clouds or haze, and the moon is barely a thumbnail, so the night sky is nice and black. We put a large rug out on the deck, lay on our backs to have a straight-up view, and screamed every time we saw a meteor streaking across the sky. The greater the streak, the louder the screams. Maybe that's why Cousin Junior checked on us. My hope is that my 2 granddaughters will never forget our Girls Day meteors, and will invest our time together in their memory banks.

All too quickly, Girls Day was over. To make it last just a little longer, we went back to the rusty and dusty store for some last minute admiring. The girls were leaving as Hubby was arriving. He had agreed to meet us there so that I would have a ride back to the cabin. It was awfully sweet of him to let me ride with him since I wouldn't let him participate in Girls Day.

As soon as we said our goodbyes, which takes our family about a half hour, Hubby and I went into the rusty and dusty store and got a lot of Christmas shopping done. He fixed the round bottom on the rusty watering can so that it sits properly and doesn't rock. I really, really hope my daughters liked all those little things they kept touching, because all those little things will be under the tree this year.

TROPICAL STORM ZETA

Dear Jennifer,

How do people in Florida deal with hurricanes? Tropical storm Zeta was enough to convince me that I'm as far south and east as I need to go. The wind here was ferocious. And poor Hubby had just gotten up all the leaves the day before. There were more leaves on the ground after Zeta than Hubby had raked up earlier. I was working away at my laptop answering emails and the power flickered. That's always a bad sign. Sure enough, at 10:30 a.m., the power went off completely. Our neighborhood is always the last to have our power restored. The electric company wants to get big neighborhoods up and running to make a bigger impact. Our neighborhood consists of one short street and a cul-de-sac, so we all have generators. The rich neighbors down the street have a generator that automatically kicks in. Ours is the kind you have to lug out of the garage, fill with fuel, and haul to the back porch. So we always give the electric company a few hours to get it fixed before we go to a lot of trouble.

At 3:00 we figured we were on our own, so we moved the car out of the garage to get to the generator. But wait. Now would be a good time to sweep this part of the garage. Hubby is a now person and I have learned over the years to just grin and bear it. I realize that I'm a 'not now' person, so at least when we do things his way, things really do get done. If you were to walk into our garage, you could tell at a glance whose side is whose. His side looks like a library with all his tools and equipment filed in Dewey Decimal order. My side looks like a gang of vandals came through, looking for buried treasure.

So we swept the part of the garage that hasn't been swept since the last time we got the generator out - probably after the last ice storm. It was pretty nasty back there, but there was no evidence of rotten tomato residue from that other time. Then Hubby noticed the dead bug crud on the window sills. Bugs are pretty stupid. If I were a bug trying to beat a window pane with my body, and saw all those dead bugs just below me, I would try to find another way out. I guess if you have a brain the size of a poppy seed, you don't go through that thought process. So Hubby had to clean off the garage window sills.

Eventually, we got back to the generator. Prep time took about an hour, mainly because I was dealing with someone who has to analyze Every. Single. Step. Hubby might have had an ulterior motive – if he delayed long enough, the power might come back on without having to do all that work to the generator. In the meantime, the winds and rain had caused a huge pine tree to lean precariously over the next door neighbors' house. They had moved their vehicles out of their garage and were just staring at this tree, wondering what to do next. This was a little distracting and I have A.D.D. flare-ups when I'm bored out of my mind. So I kept watching the neighbors instead of paying attention to Mr. Generator Man.

We finally got to the step where we put the gas in. The now person always has a gallon of gas sitting around for just such an emergency and he poured the gas in. Just about the time Hubby was yanking the cord to get the whole thing started, he noticed the next door neighbors' light on. Yay! I got to go back to work and Hubby had to syphon the gas *back out* of the generator because you can't leave it in there. Well, I would leave it in there, because I'm a 'not now, maybe later' person. But, if Hubby wasn't such a now person, he wouldn't have had to syphon all that gas out, would he?

I worked until 8:00 that night. By then I was beyond hungry and had entered stress-eating phase. I crammed a bunch of Lower My Cholesterol Oatmeal cookies into my mouth. If oatmeal really does lower your cholesterol, mine should be well within normal range by now.

MAN CAVE

Dear Jennifer,

When Cousin Ambrose offered to drive us through Sasquatch's gun cabinet one time, I thought he was kidding. But I should've remembered that everything regarding Sasquatch is larger than life.

As it turns out, Sasquatch has a barn, part of which is gun cabinet. And since it's a barn I really can drive through it. If I wanted to, which I do not.

This barn will eventually be the ultimate man cave. It is still a work in progress. Currently, it houses a couple of recliners, shag rug, a refrigerator, snacks, crates of soda, freezers (loaded with wild game, not green beans and frozen casseroles), guns, fishing poles, and various pieces of equipment necessary to support the hunting/fishing lifestyle to which Sasquatch has grown accustomed over the years. It even has heating and air. And mounted deer heads, stuffed dead animals, turkey fans and hides of various and sundry species. If I ever decide on a career in taxidermy, I'm moving close to Sasquatch's house.

The gun cabinet, with contents included, is probably worth more than my first house. I really don't get it. If I were going to blow that much money, it would be on furniture which was manufactured in the same decade in which I am now living, not the eclectic stuff that my house is furnished with. Do you know who coined the phrase 'eclectic'? The person who thought 'out of style' had a negative connotation. I think its original etymology is Greek for 'I don't want to hurt your feelings, but are you waiting for the 70s to come back again?'

Sasquatch is missing a key ingredient in his man cave: a TV. I think he is waiting for a TV that's roughly the same dimensions as the barn door. I've been wondering how Mrs. Sasquatch puts up with his sporting excesses. But it occurred to me the other day - Sasquatch is NOT in the house. He is NOT dropping potato chip crumbs between the cushions. His sweet tea glass is NOT leaving a ring on the end table. And he is NOT decorating the house in his particular style of … uh … animal and earth tones.

Now I'm beginning to wonder if I should start pushing for Hubby to get plumbing and refrigeration down in his barn. It already has heat. The only other thing missing is eclectic furniture and I know just where he can find some.

AND AWAY WE GO

Dear Jennifer,

This is my topmost, best kept, worst secret. You know by now that it is one of those 'read now and chew up later' letters. My family has been laughing at this for years, so why shouldn't you?

When we first inherited our mountain property we only had a camper trailer to stay in. It was a nice 29-foot trailer with a slide out and was roomy enough to enjoy a weekend stay without getting in each other's way. Camper trailers that size are always advertised as being able to sleep 6, but trust me, by the time you bring your groceries and clothes for the weekend inside that trailer, it shrinks up to 'sleeps 2 – 3' if one of you is a small child.

We used that trailer for 15 years before beginning construction on our cabin. We were very unhappy to see it go when we moved into the 'big house', which doesn't sleep as many as the trailer claimed.

Hubby kept that trailer in pristine condition. He saw to regular maintenance on the A/C and plumbing, kept the roof sealed, constantly patrolled for critters who wanted to camp with us – that sort of thing. As we were in the middle of nowhere, we didn't have the luxury of a septic tank or a dumping station, so Hubby proclaimed his 'no solid waste' rule. Anyone who has ever had to empty the waste water at a campsite would appreciate this rule. We have known too many fellow campers who had to take a long emergency shower after taking down their trailers for the weekend on account of the little waste problem. It is never a good 'last memory' of one's vacation.

Our 'no solid waste' rule was diligently followed, mainly because violators had to pay by cleaning out the sewer hose at take down time.

You might be wondering what we were to do because Nature still called while we were staying right in the middle of all that nature. The problem was simply solved by having a powder room located 15 feet away from the trailer. It consisted of a plastic toilet ring which snapped onto a folding seat like a director's chair. Attached to this was a black lawn and leaf bag. The great outdoors served as the walls and roof. It was not uncomfortable unless the weather was bad. My ancestors preferred the 'acting branch' but that was another era. And you probably never considered the fact that an outhouse can look pretty welcoming given the right circumstances.

Sometimes I managed to be visiting Cousin Ambrose or Cousin Junior when I was expecting Nature to call. I'm sure they didn't mind; after all, they are both still speaking to me. But even if I didn't have a handy cousin to visit, our powder room had the best views of any loo in existence. Every now and then, though, things went awry.

This tale is going to be about one of those 'awry' times. One day I simply had to go and there were no handy cousins to visit. I began to wonder what the view would be like from further up the hill as I sat and pondered life's mysteries (where do all my pens go, how do you pick a good watermelon, etc.). So I took the little folding seat with black lawn and leaf bag up the hill.

I was right about one thing – the view was pretty awesome from my new vantage point. But I was only right about one thing.

There I was enjoying Nature's beauty all around me, free of any obstructions such as walls or ceiling, and free of any shorts because they were gathered around my ankles. If I had paid more attention in physics class, I might have remembered that Isaac Newton said something about gravity which, in today's vernacular, goes something like: a pudgy girl parked on a lightweight collapsible folding chair at a steep angle on the side of a hill will not stay parked for long and silly girls who think otherwise are headed down the hill.

Which I was and backwards and with my shorts gathered around my ankles. But Newton and I weren't finished. I gained momentum. That might be another one of his laws that I broke. I didn't make straight A's in physics. All I know is – I was rolling end over end down a steep hill and gaining speed with every rotation. And I'll let you in on another little secret: whoever said it doesn't roll uphill knew exactly what they were talking about.

Fortunately, my trip down the hillside was cut short by a well-placed large fallen log. Unfortunately, my position at the time of my sudden termination was such that my lips landed up close and personal with the base of the log and my ankles and shorts went on over to see what was on the other side. I seriously can't remember where my arms went. Wherever they had chosen to go was the wrong location because I needed them to remove myself from this log. Have you ever seen those boxes that say 'This End Up'? Well … mine was.

What I do remember is that when the laughing hyenas I call my family ran to my rescue, it took them too long to compose themselves to be of any assistance and I had to figure out things on my own.

The laughing continued off and on for days. Finally, it subsided. Not long ago, I asked Hubby how long they actually laughed at me. His answer: "Well, let me think … so far, it has been 17 years.

OUR FAVORITE FAST FOOD CHICKEN PLACE

Dear Jennifer,

Sometimes on our way to the mountains we stop at the local Fast Food Chicken place for a weekend's worth of chicken for Hubby. A small portion of that is also our lunch. We have done this enough times to have a bit of a routine going, but it is still a very awkward activity. Hubby backs into a very scenic space in the parking lot (we are still careful about Covid germs and avoid public dining rooms whenever possible) while I pull out the necessary items. We call this our truck picnic, which is quite fun when you don't get out much. If you order a twelve-piece special, you get to choose three sides. We usually get fries, and a couple of other non-important things. We start with the fries. Well, duh. Our theory is that you can't eat those fries after they have cooled off. The fries are in a very large container - I would say it holds about three regular servings. We manage to make it two servings - 10 fries for me, and 60 fries for Hubby. This local Fast Food Chicken place ranks near the top in the fries category on my fast food ratings chart.

Meanwhile, as Hubby and I are busy consuming fries before they lose their tongue-burn status, I am holding the box on my lap. In case you haven't seen the box, it is large enough to hold a smaller box containing twelve pieces of chicken, another box containing six biscuits, the remaining two containers of sides and a half-gallon of tea. When the big box is empty I use it to haul all my recyclables to the dump. I hope I have given you enough information to understand how awkward this setup is and how cumbersome that box is. And it can be really hot on my lap with all that chicken inside. Oh, and Hubby always buys me a medium sweet tea with extra, extra lemon because I am too much of a lady to drink it directly from the jug. And I could do that, only there wouldn't be a good tea-to-lemon ratio this way. If I can't have lemon,

I'm simply not interested in the tea. Also, we don't have a straw that long ...

Once the fries are totally consumed, Hubby is ready for his second course, which is a piece of chicken, and he usually has a drumstick because he is too full from all those fries to eat anything larger. He usually stands outside of the truck to eat his chicken to prevent crumbs from falling all over everything. He is a very tidy person. I don't have to bother with standing in the parking lot because I can eat my crumby chicken right over the box since it's sitting on my lap.

Now that we are mostly satisfied that the food was good and we aren't going to starve for another few minutes, I get out of the truck, taking the box with me, load the tea and 2 remaining sides in the cooler on the backseat, and try to fit the future recycles box in the back floorboard. I know what you're thinking: why didn't she do that in the first place? Because the temperature of those fries continues to drop while we wait for me to get comfortable and they are better if consumed immediately.

And that's how we usually do a local Fast Food Chicken lunch, which is exactly how we did it last Friday, only the girl at the window informed us that I couldn't have extra, extra lemon for my medium sweet tea because I got the only slice they had left. Wh-a-a-at? Is that even possible? In times like these, you can easily sort the lemon-lovers from the people with absolutely no taste. I was preparing to march into that establishment and demand my lemon rights. You know I am normally a sweetie, but I have my limits. And tea without the proper quantity of lemon is my limit. Hubby stopped me from going inside and embarrassing him, and possibly getting us barred from future visits.

We got to the cabin and Cousin Ambrose was waiting with a bucket of lemons for me. He has his own tree. Hubby said that surely God has a sense of humor. I was fussing over not getting two slices of lemon and there were forty lemons waiting for me at the cabin. And they are really, really good in a glass of local Fast Food Chicken Place sweet tea.

BEAU AND INDO

Dear Jennifer,

I think I've told you about my neighbors, the Hendersons, Eloise and Theodore. They have a petting farm – meaning that their animals are there as pets, not for work – which includes a horse, donkey, geese, dogs and a couple of cats. The cats stay in a heated utility room and a possum cuddles up with then on cold evenings, but I don't think they count the possum as one of their pets. They probably should, because they are buying it cat food, whether they realize it or not. We love living next door to them, especially when the grandsweeties come over. They think we are treating them to a real petting zoo when we take them next door for a visit.

Their latest acquisition is a cockatiel. His name is Beau and he is quite smart. Hubby taught him *Fisher's Hornpipe*. Now whenever we go next door, when Hubby walks in, Beau starts whistling *Fisher's Hornpipe*. Then Hubby joins in. They whistle quite well together. Hubby whistles more on key, but Beau dances while he whistles. Currently, they are working on two-part harmony. After the performance Beau flies around the room and gets friendly with someone. Last week it was me. There I was with a pretty Beau in my hair. And don't think I wasn't praying mightily. Don't worry – I didn't have to wash my hair when I got home.

Recently the Hendersons had their hands full with two family members in two different hospitals in two different counties. So they asked us to let the dogs out. Fortunately, we didn't have to care for the other animals. That would have required some serious note taking before the Hendersons left the house.

Letting the dogs out seemed to be an easy chore. I had mucked the horse stall for them a few years before and it was not a chore I wanted to repeat. Note – stall mucking doesn't require serious note taking. There's the pitchfork. Now, get busy. That's about all there is to it.

Hubby and I went over to let Baxter and Dixie run around, sniff, and do their thing, but we were a little surprised to see a third dog - Indo. Indo is the Henderson's granddog and is about the same size as Dixie and Baxter: 20+ pounds. Indo didn't know us or care to know us, and certainly didn't want to go outside for us. We had to remove ourselves from the doorway so that Indo would stop thinking whatever it is that dogs think when strangers stand between them and the great outdoors. Finally we had all three dogs outside.

Dixie came right back in. She can't see well anymore, so she hangs near Baxter, which is fine until Baxter wants to explore. So we had two dogs outside and one inside. Baxter got finished doing his business and came inside. One dog outside and two inside. Indo wasn't planning to come in. We were trying too hard to get him to come in and he wasn't cooperating. We begged. We whistled. We made all those friendly 'come here' noises. Indo wasn't stupid. It was time to use the magic word: TREAT! Dixie came out. Baxter came out. Indo ran further away from us. Three dogs outside. Around this time Hubby and I started calling this dog In-don't. So I went inside to get the treat jar. Baxter and Dixie led the way because they know where the treat jar is. One dog outside and two inside.

The treat jar was empty. This bears repeating. THE TREAT JAR WAS EMPTY. I looked in all the cabinets, the pantry, even the fridge. No treats. Dixie gave up on me and went back to the master bedroom. I hope that was okay because she really likes their comforter. Baxter was ready. He was doing all the cute tricks he usually does to get his treat. What a waste of his time. And I looked like a liar to this sweet little dog because I did say the 'T' word. So I went back to the fridge. I was too desperate to get the cereal and crackers out of the pantry. This job called for hot dogs, which I just happened to notice in the fridge. I didn't care that hot dogs might be on the meal plan for that night. Humans' dinner was going to be someone else's problem.

Baxter knew what a hot dog is. He ramped up his game. More

tricks. Cuter face. Dainty little whine. This dog knows how to earn treats. So I made a deal with him. "Baxter, if you will help me get Indo to come inside, I'll give you most of this hot dog". You know you've reached the outer edges of frustration when you start bargaining with a dog. Baxter and I went outside to lure Indo in. Two dogs outside and one inside. I broke the hot dog in little bites. There were only three hot dogs in the fridge, so I had limited resources to make this work. Indo seemed interested. Poor Baxter. He did everything but tap dance with a straw hat and cane. I gave Baxter a bite of hot dog to show Indo the riches that could be his.

Then I encouraged Baxter to go inside and prayed that Indo would follow, which he finally did. Three dogs inside. Pure joy! After I gave Baxter a generous portion of hot dog for being my very capable assistant (don't ever tell Baxter, but they were turkey dogs), I went straight home, jumped in the car, went to the store and bought two 60-ounce boxes of dog biscuits. That was the largest size they had. I did not buy hot dogs. The next time our pet sitting services are required, I'm going to sign up for stall mucking. It doesn't take as long, I don't require an assistant, and I have everyone's cooperation.

MORE KUDZU

Dear Jennifer,

Last weekend we made a final sweep across the kudzu before it dies back for the year. Our latest attempt was attacking *up* from the roadside instead of *down* from the woods. The problem with working along the roadside is, well, it's on the side of the road. It's a one-lane road and the drivers of pickups and canoe trailers come zipping around the curves like they own the road. Sometimes there is a shoulder where we can stand away from the traffic and sometimes there isn't. We have learned to take a dive down the embankment when the need arises. My old P.E. teacher wouldn't believe it. Hubby would prefer to leave the kudzu on the road bank but I am determined to totally eradicate it, destroy it, terminate it, and use any other verb that means 'get rid of it'. Hubby can be very accommodating, mainly because it's just less trouble and eventually, my complaining about kudzu will wear him down anyway.

So there we were, using the kudzu vines as rope – they do have some benefit – and inching our way up the steep, slippery bank. It was then that Hubby noticed the fresh deer carcass in the ditch. Apparently, the driver of a pickup truck or a canoe trailer came around the curve too fast. That deer should've headed down the embankment like we do. I couldn't gag because I needed to concentrate on not sliding back down the steep, slippery bank and landing on the dead deer. I will spare you any further disgusting details. Let me just say that every kudzu vine we dug up became a shroud for the deer. I might have even stopped working sooner than planned because I know how my luck usually goes. And it never ends pretty.

YUMMY VEGGIE BURGERS

Dear Jennifer,

As you know, my life is very busy during the week, so if I want anything to eat, I have to cook it on the weekends or consume fast food all week. Fast food is okay, but there again, I don't have time to go to Weight Watchers after eating all that fast food. So last weekend I made a batch of veggie burgers. I had packed up all my ingredients to take with me to the cabin and it was a good day for staying indoors. It was cold outside and the wind was so ferocious even the remaining kudzu had trouble holding on.

Anyway, I was mixing and stirring and mashing away in my little kitchen. I had black beans, rice, zucchini, corn, spinach, garlic, onions, oatmeal, chili powder, salt, taco seasoning and an egg to hold it all together in a large mixing bowl. It looked like a great recipe coming together. You can always tell – every single kitchen gadget was dirty except for the pizza cutter. Everything was going smoothly until I got to the flavor/texture builder section of the recipe.

I had no flax seed. I always use flax seed. I checked the fridge. Not there. I was sure I had packed it. I checked the big box that travels back and forth to the mountains with me. Not there. I checked my list of flavor/texture builder choices for a reasonable substitute: chopped sun dried tomatoes (don't like them), chopped fresh herbs (didn't have any), sesame seeds (fresh out), mashed avocado (nope), tahini (too expensive), chopped nuts (I don't think so), unsweetened nut butter (yuck). I was supposed to pick 2. There were some old walnuts in the fridge. I seriously didn't want walnuts in my veggie burgers but I was short on options. I had to choose 2 flavor/texture builders so I was forced to use chopped walnuts and store brand peanut butter, which wasn't unsweetened, by the way. But I was desperate.

So I stirred all my ingredients together and then cleaned off an area to start shaping patties. I put away the eggs, the flax seed, the spices … wait … what? There was a bag of flax seed right in front of me and I couldn't find it 5 minutes before I dumped peanut butter and walnuts in my veggie burgers? Well, this is a batch that will have 3 flavor/texture builders instead of 2. I threw that flax seed right in there with the walnuts and peanut butter.

Actually, the burgers tasted pretty good. When topped with a thick slice of tomato, a thick slice of Vidalia onion, lettuce, pickles, banana peppers and cheese on a big fat sesame seed bun dowsed with mustard, ketchup and mayo, you would hardly know there is no meat in there. Oh, and you have to like the taste of beans, but other than that, they really are good.

SEASONAL WREATH

Dear Jennifer,

I am not much of a decorator, mainly because I am cheap and I don't want to waste money on décor that goes out of style, and then has to be replaced with new stuff that I have to spend more money on. It's an endless cycle. Nevertheless, I do hang a seasonal wreath next to the front door on the cabin, mainly because the cabin is plain and brown and needs a little something to keep it from looking too drab. Logs make a cabin look cute and cozy, but they are very boring. The way I save money on this is to use one wreath all year. Every few months I take everything off the wreath from the season before and freshen it up with whatever colors and flowers happen to be in vogue for the current season. This is also a good way to save space. Our cabin is snug and cozy, which are realtor words for 'tight spaces', so storage space is at a premium and wreaths are bulky.

I bought an old milk can a few years ago because it had a timeless beauty, which are realtor words for 'ugly and completely out of style'. But it reminded me of the days when Granny Carmen strained the milk into one of these cans every morning and Grandpa Daniel took it down to the road to wait for the milkman to pick it up. I wonder if the milk ever spoiled. That will have to be another story.

This milk can is rusty and has been painted over and is a little beaten up. Timeless beauty. And the black paint is peeling off. No one will ever steal this can off my porch. And that's a good thing, because it has a practical use. At the cabin everything has to be useful or it doesn't get to stay. There is no room for a pretty little gewgaw that can't carry its weight. My milk can holds all the little silk flowers that go on my wreath and are waiting their turn for whatever season they happen to represent. Every season of silk flowers is sealed securely in a zippered plastic bag to keep its contents free from dust, peeling paint, or bug ammunition.

This year has been a little different. I noticed a lot of bird activity on the porch in early September, but I didn't pay a lot of attention. It was way past baby bird time so I knew the birds weren't building this time of year. If it were spring, Hubby would be on bird patrol making sure the birds weren't in construction phase. In the spring, he is out there putting old drink cans along the eaves to keep the birds from building there. The birds love our eaves, but they don't love drink cans. They don't like the shiny aluminum and it scares them. It is a little embarrassing when we have guests on the porch and they look up and see Coke cans looking back down at them. Then we have to explain. It is easier to explain Coke cans than it is to scrape bird stuff off the eaves every week-end.

So I thought it was too late in the year for nest building, but I was mistaken. A chickadee couple chose my summer wreath to be their home. How irritating. By the time I started paying attention it was too late. My summer wreath with its colorful flowers and greenery was adorned with a bird's nest. The birds actually did a good job and positioned their nest directly in the center of the flower arrangement, making it very decorative. It looks like a florist created this work of art. Of course, a florist wouldn't poop on a wreath, so there you are.

I actually had to lay out cash for a new wreath. I certainly wasn't going to try to hose down the icky one. Not only am I cheap, but I'm also lazy. I'm actually lazier than cheap, which is how paying for a new wreath won out over cleaning the old one. And I've waited so long that now I'm just skipping right over fall and putting a Christmas wreath on the porch. But first I will have to take the nasty (or 'nesty') wreath down.

The spring wreath is going to be a challenge. Those birds are coming back and will want to rebuild their nest as before. It will be difficult to decide how I want this wreath to look: should I allow the birds to decorate it their way or go with Hubby's décor and use shiny Coke cans?

THANKSGIVING WITH THE FAMILY

Dear Jennifer,

I always try to beat the Thanksgiving surge at the grocery store and buy the bulk of my groceries a week or two before the madness begins. This year was no different. I came home from the store feeling rather proud of myself and a little smug. Imagine all those poor shoppers waiting in that long line the night before Thanksgiving when they could be home doing food prep. I got home and sorted my supplies out by location – these go to Bea's house for lunch, these stay here for dinner with the relatives (not that we will be hungry, it's just tradition). I just love organization.

Then a couple of the relatives called up the night before Thanksgiving (while I was in the kitchen doing food prep and the last minute shoppers were standing in line at the store) and said they wouldn't be able to make it. They had made other plans with some friends. Really? You are just now finding this out? You couldn't call two weeks ago before I bought extra green beans? Did you forget your lessons in etiquette? You already accepted our invitation and you will have to tell those friends of yours that you are expected at the in-laws' house. It didn't happen. They had fun with their friends and I won't have to buy green beans again until Valentine's Day.

There were several years when my parents and my sister's family gathered together with us for Thanksgiving. It was a lot of fun, as long as all the cooks recognized my mom as the Kitchen General. This was fine with me because the General brought most of the food. It's a mom thing.

Mom and Dad would arrive early on Thanksgiving morning and haul in several boxes of supplies. We never knew why Mom brought enough food for an army when there were so few of us. Maybe the thought of all those delicious leftovers appealed to her.

The men would go into the living room and talk politics. Why couldn't they watch football like other guys do at Thanksgiving? Football isn't as rough and tumble as a political discussion. Meanwhile, the womenfolk equally divided the work in the kitchen under the General's watchful eye. My job was mainly to put ice in glasses and pour tea, basically, just stay out of the way. My sister Zuzu had the job of buttering the tops of the rolls, basically, just stay out of the way. Mom had the rest: slicing turkey, mashing potatoes, heating casseroles, making stuffing, assembling salad and making gravy.

Let's talk about gravy. It's warm, creamy, and loaded with carbs. And spooned over mashed potatoes, stuffing and biscuits, gravy is just about nature's most nearly perfect food. When I was younger and didn't have to worry so much about my weight, I would put turkey, potatoes and stuffing on my plate and cover the whole thing with gravy. Come to think of it, now that I am older I still do that. I am in charge of the gravy when we celebrate Thanksgiving at Bea's house. My family loves my special gravy recipe and I'll share it with you. It's at the grocery store on the shelves with sauce packets and jars. You can buy the chicken flavor or the turkey flavor – I can't tell the difference in the taste. It comes in a glass jar with a screw top, so that when you are preparing Thanksgiving dinner, you just pour it into a pan on top of the stove. When dinner is over, you can pour the leftovers back into the jar. This is very handy for reheating when you are ready to spoon it over what I like to call The Leftover Turkey Potato Stuffing sandwich next time you eat, which is usually two days later.

That was a nice break; now let's get back to Mom's gravy. She always came prepared with the ingredients already measured and ready to add to the skillet. My job was to get the cast iron skillet out of the cabinet. This is a pretty big skillet and very heavy. It stays at the bottom of my stack of pans so that it won't crush any of my other pieces of cookware.

One particular Thanksgiving it was down to gravy time. We all started getting excited because that meant dinner was almost ready. I pulled out the cast iron skillet with both hands and set it on top of the stove. Mom added the fat and flour and began to whisk. She appointed me to find the 'big bowl'. I got the biggest bowl in the house which is practically large enough to hold a small child. All the decorating magazines show a pretty little gravy boat on a beautiful Thanksgiving table. All of us consider that dinky little gravy boat to be a single serving. Mom's gravy required a cruise ship. Mom started adding the milk as she whisked.

The skillet is heavy enough all by itself, but when your mama makes enough gravy to feed the entire neighborhood, it weighs quite a bit more. Mom always needed my dad's help holding the skillet and tipping it toward the bowl so that she could scrape the gravy out of the pan. Dad came into the kitchen grabbed two pot holders, and began to do his job. As dad tipped the skillet for mom to scrape out the gravy, she sensed that her directions were not being followed somewhere in the vicinity of the dining room and walked away. She appeared to be checking on a minor detail, like a vegetable. Unfortunately, she failed to communicate her change of plans to Dad, who had already committed to lifting and tipping. Gravy was going into the bowl, somehow without Mom's help, but Dad knew a disaster was looming. He was trying to get her attention while still holding and tipping. There was so much gravy in the pan, it was too much for the largest bowl in the house, and gravy began spilling over the sides, onto the countertop, and down the front of the cabinet doors.

Finally, Dad had Mom's attention, but it was too late. She dashed back over to the stove and tried to help, but it was out of their hands, out of the skillet, and out of the bowl. My dad, bless his heart, was just a tad bit irritated. We never did find out what was so compelling across the room.

There was still plenty of gravy to go around, so that was no big deal. And clean-up wasn't so bad either, because all that gravy ran straight down into the heat vent. For a couple of months after that incident, we had little reminders of Thanksgiving Day every time the furnace came on. There was a delicious hint of gravy wafting through the air. It was a little disappointing when all that gravy eventually dried up. What a pleasant air freshener it made.

SMOKE ALARM

Dear Jennifer,

Hubby got a little dose of what it's like to be me the other night. First of all, you need to know that we sleep in separate rooms. There are several good reasons for this:

a. I go to bed early; he stays up until after midnight. It wakes me up when he comes to bed.
b. I get up an hour before he does and he can't sleep through shower noises.
c. I get up twice at night to go you-know-where. He gets up twice at night to go you-know-where. We can't seem to time these visits together.
d. We are on different snoring cycles.

You can see that when we sleep in the same room we get up multiple times a night, so we get along much better if we have our own rooms. So, the other night at the cabin, Hubby was going to bed around midnight when he heard a little 'beep' from the smoke alarm in his room. He waited for a few minutes to see if it would 'beep' again, and it didn't, so he went to bed. He was sleeping peacefully (because I wasn't in the room with him doing c or d from the list above) when around 1:30 a.m. he heard another 'beep' from the smoke alarm. He seriously didn't want to get up to fix it, because this one was located higher up the wall than the last smoke alarm which required battery replacement. And this one began beeping every 30 seconds, so he did have to get up and he hoped he was alert enough to get it right. He knew that he was not going to get any sleep until he got the job done.

I was asleep in the loft (I call it my cozy tree house – my favorite place on earth) so Hubby crept around very softly so as to not wake me. Isn't he a darlin'? Hubby's room has a vaulted ceiling so the smoke alarm is just below the peak of the ceiling – not possible for him to reach the alarm even when standing on a bar stool. Hubby knew this for a fact because he tried that first. Then he decided to move enough furniture to position a bookshelf under the smoke alarm. This is a bookshelf we had to put together ourselves from a kit and I am very impressed that it held up. Hubby had some difficulty moving the bookshelf under the smoke alarm at 1:35 in the morning and staying quiet enough to keep from waking me up. As I said – he's a darlin'. Finally, he reached the alarm and took out the battery, waited a few seconds, and didn't hear a beep. He was very relieved. Now he could get some sleep. Then it beeped. Without a battery.

Next, he took the alarm off the wall, disconnecting it from the power, and it beeped again. How was this thing still beeping with no battery or electricity? In desperation he hid it in his closet under his sweaters. It still beeped and he could still hear it. His next step was to take it downstairs and out the front door. And I was still sleeping like a baby. No, babies pee in the bed and cry all night. I was sleeping really well.

The alarm was out on the porch and Hubby was comfortably in bed, feeling pretty satisfied that he hadn't woken me up. Then he heard it again. Beep. It finally dawned on him that there was another alarm going off somewhere else in the house. He tiptoed around the cabin and found it in my mom's room, or the room she uses when she joins us in the mountains. Fortunately, her ceiling is a reasonable height so Hubby climbed up on the kitchen stepstool and took the alarm off the wall. Also, fortunately, my mom wasn't with us, otherwise, Hubby would've had to wake me to go to her room and wake her so that he could get the alarm off her wall without giving her a heart attack. I think Mom's alarm may have joined the other alarm out on the front porch. Or maybe up in the treetops where Hubby probably threw the other one in anger and frustration.

He finally got everything silenced and checked on me before he got back in bed at 2:15. The only noise he heard was a soft "z-z-z" (see d from the list above). I always thought I was a light sleeper. I wonder what else goes on around the house at night while I'm 'out'. I'm just glad that something weird happened to Hubby instead of me for a change.

HUBBY'S CATCH OF THE DAY

Dear Jennifer,

Last Friday Hubby and I went to the mountains and did a little end of season kudzu fighting. This last batch was on the steep road bank. I have mentioned the road bank and its dangers before. Hubby 'roped' me into getting tied up so I wouldn't fall down onto the big rocks and ultimately, the road. This is the rope that goes on forever, so Hubby had one end tied to the golf cart and the other end tied to me, of course. In between, the rope was wrapped around several trees to take up the slack. There were a lot of trees involved because there was a whole lot of slack. Our woods looked like a theater with roped off lines guiding fans in to see a blockbuster movie. Nobody was lined up in our woods to pull kudzu vines.

I was glad I was securely fastened because when I slid down so far to grab one elusive vine, there was nothing to hold my foot in place and I kept sliding. I never knew I could do a split like that. Too bad my jeans couldn't do the same. Hubby helped pull me in. He has wanted to use the golf cart to rescue me for a long time. It looked like he had landed the big one. I wonder if you have to have some sort of license for catching pudgy old ladies. Are we in season this time of year? People are so friendly in our part of the county. They are always smiling, waving, and giving us a 'thumbs up' as they drive past. Anyway, it was the first time I have traveled by golf cart while 50 feet away from the seat.

And now I know a shortcut to Cousin Ambrose's house if I'm ever in the woods and in a hurry. And if I don't mind having weeds, leaves, and sticks in my hair when I show up at his door. He lives a half mile away by truck, but only 200 yards away straight down the hill by rope. Cousin Ambrose pulled up in his truck as we were pulling vines off the bank and ropes off my body (and weeds, leaves, and sticks out of my hair). We chatted with him for a few minutes. He had a kitchen sink in the truck bed. I thought of a cute joke, but he was in aggravated plumber mode, so I kept it to myself.

On Sunday morning Sasquatch went hunting. Before daylight. He fired off several rapid shots in the pre-dawn hours. If we hadn't set our clocks back the night before I might have been annoyed, but my body just assumed it was a work day and didn't allow me to go back to sleep. Sasquatch had hit his target: a large black bear. I wonder if Mrs. Sasquatch has a collection of bear meat recipes (bear stew, bear and dumplings, barbecued bear ribs, etc.). I wonder if Mrs. Sasquatch ever gets to cook 'normal' foods like chicken, or a hamburger made with beef from a cow. I wonder if she has regular draperies, or drapes made from skins. I wonder if they will ever invite us over so I can check on these things.

Anyway, Sasquatch was like a little kid showing off his new toy. He sent us pictures. Lots and lots of pictures. He posed with the bear (he and the bear were roughly the same size). He took a picture of the bear's paw resting in his paw (also roughly the same size). Then he sent a shot taken from an angle that nice ladies shouldn't look at, so I looked away. I have no way of knowing for sure, but those babies are probably NOT the same size.

OUTDOOR CHRISTMAS TREE

Dear Jennifer,

Last weekend at the cabin we decided to get our outdoor tree ready for Christmas lights. We do things the hillbilly way up there: we leave the lights on the tree all year long. The reason for this is simple. It's too cold to take the lights down in January, February, or March, and by then the leaves are starting to come out and the lights are sort of forgotten. As a result, after two years of this, all the lights had sort of slid around and bunched up in one location. And guess what? We had to take them down anyway to test them. One string was half lit and half burned out. The other string was burned out on each end and lit in the middle. They're both at the county landfill now. We suspected it would be this way so we had 150 feet of new lights ready to string on our tree.

We also had six of those balls made from chicken wire and covered with lights, like those on display in Sunset Hills in Greensboro. If you have never been through that neighborhood during the Christmas season, I hope you can try to go. The lights are breathtaking. There are thousands of them and this isn't one of those times that I am exaggerating. Our six measly balls aren't breathtaking, but you have to start somewhere. I plan to eventually work up to breathtaking on our mountain. The trick will be how to get Hubby to shoot drop cords through the trees for me.

The six chicken wire balls looked pretty rough. Five of them still lit up, although the colors had chipped off most bulbs. Ball number six was on the ground under a pile of leaves. It had been flattened by a fallen tree limb last summer. It was no longer a ball - more like a pizza. The lights were dead so I peeled those off, pulled the chicken wire back into a roundish shape, and got most of the twigs and leaves out of it. It had suffered so. Then it got a new set of lights and is now brightly hanging on the tree, which looks kind of odd since the other five balls don't really have colors anymore.

My sweet engineer/mathematician insisted on stringing the lights in a triangular shape as his base. I can't tell you how many times I got slapped in the face with pine boughs trying to help him achieve this effect. But it smelled good. Eventually he was satisfied. I never understood the need for a perfect triangle, but this whole outdoor tree thing is mostly for him, so I tried very hard to keep my comments to myself. Very hard. Very. Very. Hard. Every time I thought it looked fine, he noticed a spot that wasn't true to triangle form. While he was inspecting, it was my job to crawl up and in between all those limbs and make the necessary adjustments. Standing at my full 5'2" I had to use whatever tools I had, and a large rock was nearby, so I was able to stand on it to reach the higher branches. But at some point I made a misstep and started falling backwards. This probably does not surprise you.

Now might be the time to tell you that my mom finds beauty in old dead tree trunks. She likes to display them as a focal point in a flower bed. I guess they're alright if you consider a thick chunk of wood with roots sticking out all over to be pretty. I should also tell you that I gave her a plot of ground to call her own and plant flowers there. Her flower garden, complete with a decorative dead tree trunk, is very pretty in the summer and fall months and is positioned right beside Hubby's Christmas tree.

And now, back to our story. I started falling backwards. And there, right in my line of fire, was that dead tree trunk with several dangerous roots sticking out from it at all angles. I was headed for an immediate and painful colonoscopy without the benefit of anesthesia. Fortunately, my survival gene kicked in and I had the presence of mind to grab onto a couple of pine branches which were very sturdy. And sticky. I was spared a trip to the ER and having to explain why there were tree roots stuck up my derrière.

At night time the Christmas tree looks very pretty, which is really all that matters. And after four showers I still have sticky pine sap on my fingers, arms and neck and little pieces of pine bark in my underwear. I don't know how I got coated with tree bark, but when your life is passing before your eyes and wooden prongs are threatening to alter your seating arrangements, I guess some important details can get overlooked.

CHRISTMAS BRUNCH

Dear Jennifer,

Last Saturday was our family's Christmas get-together. We celebrate the Saturday before Christmas unless that happens to be Christmas Eve, in which case we celebrate the Saturday before that, OR unless Covid makes everybody do ridiculous things, in which case we have to have a Zoom Christmas, which we did last year and I didn't get to see my babies, but I did get to see Sasquatch, which was not the same thing as seeing my babies, and this has become a run-on sentence.

So last Saturday we felt that we should have double fun to make up for the Christmas lost to Covid last year. We always have brunch and this year was no exception. I was in charge of eggs, biscuits, three pounds of bacon and two pounds of sausage. I could cook twelve pounds of bacon and we would run out. I thought three pounds was enough to enjoy and still not clog the arteries of my sons (in-law). Hubby has stated that if, when he gets to Heaven, he finds out that bacon was good for him, he is going to be really mad.

Ellen and Jarrod were in charge of the grits bar. A grits bar is perfectly acceptable in the South and I am surprised it hasn't become more popular. Jarrod made a three-quart crock pot full of grits for a dozen people. He wanted to be sure we didn't run out of grits. To make it a full grits bar, he brought another pound each of crumbled bacon and sausage, sliced green onions and a gallon-size zippered bag full of shredded cheddar. And no, we didn't run out of cheddar. But we could have, so why take the risk?

One of the more health-conscious people in our family brought fruit, which was mostly ignored. If you have bacon and grapes in front of you, which are you going to pick?

We all contributed homemade cookies for the cookie bar. Let me just say that the cookie bar might have been the best food idea I ever had. Each of us made three or four kinds of cookies which we added to the cookies our neighbors brought over. I can't wait until February. All the sugar should be out of my system by then and I won't be so hyper. It will be nice to fall asleep again.

My sweet family gathered in the living room to read the Christmas story. We start out that way every Christmas as a reminder that it all began in a stable and that the first Gift will always be the best gift.

To make the day last, we would eat a little, sing a few Christmas carols, open a couple of presents, and go back and eat a little more. After four or five rotations like this, that gallon bag of cheese didn't look so intimidating and the boys began fighting over the remaining grits. There might have been one last grit left in the bottom of the crock pot. The bacon and sausage didn't make it past the second rotation.

No one fought over the grapes. There were still plenty after we began cleaning up. "Would you like to take some of my toffee bars home?" "Oh, yes! Would you like to take some grapes?" "No, that's okay. You keep them."

LIFE WITH MOTHER

Hi, Jennifer

My mom gave us quite a scare a few weeks ago. She had appendicitis. You would think as old as her appendix is, it would be content to remain as is. But this one got ugly and mean. Mom had to stay in the hospital for a week and suffered terribly while she was there. The doctor wanted her to visit a rehab facility until she was stronger but Zuzu and I wanted to take care of her ourselves. I arranged to work remotely from Mom's house on week days and Zuzu offered to take care of her on weekends. Mom would be happier and more comfortable at home. Zuzu and I wanted to be sure that Mom fully recovered because she is the person who is going to take care of us when we get old.

I kept a daily journal of my role as caregiver.

Week 1
Monday
Mom was waiting for me in her hospital room this morning, dressed and ready to go. Fortunately, all the paperwork was completed, and Mom was actually getting to leave before lunch time. I went to the parking garage while the nurses were doing last minute checks. And one of my secret fears was realized. I couldn't find my way out of the garage. I circled my level 3 times before I realized I was going nowhere. I circled 3 more times looking for the exit signs. I finally got to the window, handed the parking attendant my ticket and she said, "Have to back up. Stick your ticket in the slot". So I did, just as quickly as possible after signaling to the driver behind me that he had to back up also. Then I pulled up and gave the parking attendant my credit card. She said, "Have to back up. It's automated". So I did, just as quickly as possible after signaling to the driver behind me that he had to back up again.

By this time I was beginning to sweat, wondering if the volunteer pushing the wheelchair had given up on me and abandoned my little mama at the curb, and wondering if I would even get there considering the driver behind me was staring at me with road rage eyes. I finally escaped that terrifying garage and went around 11 traffic circles to pick up my precious cargo. Only I didn't realize she was one driveway over. So I circled Winston-Salem and tried it again. By the time we got her loaded safely and securely in my car, I was ready for a blood pressure cuff and some strong meds. Or two cigarettes – one for each hand. And I don't smoke. Yet.

We got home without incident, which was a miracle, given the way my morning had gone. Mom was so glad to be home, she went straight to bed. I unloaded the car and left her unattended for an hour while I went to the grocery store. Oh, blessed grocery store. No backing up. No traffic circles. Just up and down, aisle after aisle. I was finally in my comfort zone. I bought chocolate chunk cookies for medicinal purposes.

The remainder of my day was spent helping Mom walk from here to there and doing the work I actually get paid to do. I am doing the work I actually get paid to do at the old desk I used to do my homework on when I was in high school, so it really is a very old desk. I sit in a ladder back chair with a thin cushion between me and some very hard wooden slats. My calculator is on a TV tray to my right. It's primitive, but it works.

Mom got so many phone calls from well-wishers during the day, she kept her hearing aids out so she could put the phone up to her ear. That's a pretty clever excuse for not wearing her hearing aids. This required listening to the TV at decibels comparable to those of a jet engine. I think I may be going deaf. Hubby and Zuzu showed up at the same time, ready for the gourmet dinner I had prepared: meatloaf. It was pretty good considering I haven't cooked in ages and I hadn't eaten in ages, either. My stress level did not allow for much food today except for a couple of chocolate chunk cookies or twelve.

Now Mom is tucked in for the night and I am in my old room, in my old bed. The bed my parents bought for Zuzu and me in

1963. I am lying on the mattress they bought for this bed in 1963. Zuzu declared that its inner workings have calcified. Every time I move, something under me crackles and breaks. It sounds like corn flakes and feels like concrete. Tomorrow night I'm going to upgrade and put a sleeping bag out on the carport floor so I can be more comfortable.

Tuesday
I woke up covered in bruises. I have an acute case of pelvic concretitis with general igneous mattressious malfunction, caused by prolonged exposure to concrete cornflakes. Mom asked me this morning how I slept. I told her just fine. She didn't believe me. She thought maybe she should switch out the mattresses since hers is getting too soft. No, no! You're a helpless invalid! Don't you want to get better? Wait. Does that mean I can sleep on your soft mattress?

Okay, enough whining about that. Today was a teensy bit better. She was more like the little mama we all know and love. She ate an entire spoonful of cereal with a fourth of a banana for breakfast. I wolfed down my breakfast muffins, the rest of Mom's banana, and whatever else was within reach. Aunt Hecuba promised to bring soup for lunch, so Mom freshened up while I did some of the work I actually get paid to do at my little old desk with accompanying TV tray. Mom wanted me to make a dessert for our lunch, so she got to boss me around in the kitchen a little. Auntie showed up with a cooler packed with lasagna, cheddar cheese muffins (my personal favorite), sausage and potato soup, ham biscuits and breakfast muffins. I may have sneaked into the kitchen several times to sample a cheddar cheese muffin.

As Auntie was leaving, the home health nurse showed up. I excused myself and went back to the den to do the work I actually get paid to do. Mom's next door neighbor Curtis walked in, asked Mom what had happened, and then sat down so he could be comfortable while he told MY MAMA'S nurse all about his aches and pains. She didn't even acknowledge his presence. She didn't even give him an 'um-hmm'. Just kept talking to Mom like they were the only 2 people in the room.

Not one to take hints, Curtis talked until he was satisfied, then left. After he left the A/C guy came. While he was working on the air, my uncle called. Now I know how an air traffic controller feels.

We spent several hours outside this afternoon. The humidity was low and there was a nice breeze. I might have dozed off a time or two. Hubby and Zuzu had supper with us, which was yesterday's leftovers, plus the dessert I had made for lunch. After supper Hubby and Zuzu left and Mom put her hearing aids to bed. I get really sad when she does this. We went into the den to watch a game show without hearing aids. She wanted to know if I could hear it. Isn't that sweet? Zuzu probably heard it across the street at her house. Then we called it a night. I took a bath in my old tub. I always thought it was bigger than that.

Wednesday
Mom went without her walker all day. She swept the carport and made a pitcher of tea. The good kind with real sugar, no sugar substitute. As soon as her extremely light lunch was over she started having reflux and her day went downhill from there. Curtis came over to tell my elderly mother who is recovering from major surgery that he has been having some trouble with his feet. The pastor came by and so did Mom's friend, Nadine. Zuzu, Hubby and I ate the lasagna Auntie had made. It was a cheese lover's dream, containing ricotta, cheddar, Swiss and Parmesan. Now I have reflux just like Mom. I did the work I actually get paid to do until 10:30 - that's pm - in anticipation of the internet guy's visit tomorrow. I am very excited about this visit. I have been working off cable for 3 days now.

Now I'm resting on the world's firmest mattress. Firm like a sidewalk.

Thursday
Bad night last night. And it was a long night. I won't get more specific than that. But my thinking is – when I was small and helpless my little mama got up with me at night. Now that she

230

is small and helpless, it's my turn to repay her. But whatever happened last night was worth it – the reflux is gone. The home health nurse came back today and told Mom that for every day she was in the hospital, it takes 3 days to recover, plus more for surgery time. I could see Mom's little math gears turning and suddenly, a light bulb went on. When the nurse left, Mom wanted fries! We have turned a corner. Cable people came and upgraded Mom's cable and installed the internet. Mostly. Now I can do the work I actually get paid to do a lot faster.

Mom's Sunday school class came for a visit and brought several boxes of food and supplies. They included paper plates and everything we needed to have a few dinners and not have to wash dishes. I love those people. Mom's Sunday school teacher always makes the best pound cakes and made one for us. I understand that his wife is a good cook as well.

Friday
The new internet and my old printer did not get along at all and cost me several extra hours of work. On the bright side, Mom is walking around and no longer looks hopeless. Hubby came to pick me up to go to the cabin and Zuzu took over babysitting duties. I feel just like a new mother leaving her baby with the sitter for the first time. Zuzu has my number if she needs anything.

LIFE WITH MOTHER II

Dear Jennifer,

I know you have been extremely antsy waiting for the next installment of Life with Mother.

Week 2
Monday
We are still eating leftovers. There are so many containers in the fridge, we make it our goal to try and empty a couple each meal. Food in larger containers gets eaten a little bit, and then is moved to smaller containers. It has been quite a challenge to fit these various sized containers together like a giant 3-D jigsaw puzzle. Unfortunately, the tangerines got pushed to the back of the fridge and I didn't see them again for days. Hubby couldn't come for dinner. Now I don't ask for much, but when I am living away from home, I want to see my man. On the bright side, Mom improves a little each day.

Tuesday
Mom fired the home health nurse. There was never such a cheerful job loss. I will miss Glynnis. If I ever need a nurse, I'm calling her. We went to the outpatient clinic to get Mom's staples and stitches removed. She felt a lot better after that. The PA was concerned about the swelling still present in Mom's feet and legs and recommended compression hose. By the way, compression hose are not cheap. A single pair costs $50. You can imagine the joy my Mom expressed over this, especially when she learned that insurance does not cover it. The PA also recommended yogurt to replace all the good bacteria Mom lost over the last 2 weeks. At the mention of yogurt, I could see Mom willing her good bacteria to come back on its own, because she was NOT eating 'that stuff'. So I wasn't stupid enough to buy any.

Wednesday
A memorable day. Our first experience with compression hose. They weren't kidding when they described these hose as

'tight'. Getting one of these on a human foot could be compared to forcing a balloon over a watermelon. Mom lay on her back in the bed and I began working the first stocking over her foot. I managed to cover 3 toes before the trouble began. Did I miss something in the instructions? Should I have stretched this apart with a vise grip first? This was like pouring a cat into a carrier, only in reverse. I fought. I struggled. I twisted. I turned. I prayed really, really hard. "Lord, please help me get this on my little mama without setting her recovery back a week."

Finally, I had Mom brace her foot on my chest and push. Perhaps I should've told her not to push so hard. You wouldn't think a little old lady recovering from major surgery would have such strength in her legs. When I picked myself up off the floor we tried it again. Only this time I told her to push *gently*. At last, we had one stocking on. But we had another leg to go. I had to sit down and rest for a few minutes before beginning with a new stocking. I tried stretching it from the bedroom door all the way down the hall to the kitchen. I don't know what sort of fabric was used in the construction of these compression hose, but I have to give it points for tenacity. It didn't go any better or any faster with leg #2. This looks like a job that doesn't improve with practice. There doesn't seem to be a trick to it, unless you choose a patient with pipe cleaner legs. I sure hope the foot-shaped indentation on my chest goes away soon. It isn't very attractive.

Thursday
Those compression hose are little miracle workers. The swelling has gone down considerably. Bea & Co. surprised Mom today and stayed for a couple of hours. Belle practiced her grin for her great-grandmama and had her in the palm of her hand. Cedric is getting too tall and too good looking. We're going to have to do something about that. After everybody left, the 2 of us actually went somewhere. We got in the car and just went for a drive, something we haven't done in years. Mom still pushes against the floorboard when she thinks I should hit the brakes sooner. She started doing this in 1971 and I doubt if she will ever change. Later in the

afternoon, Hubby took her for a ride around the neighborhood. She told him a little story about every house on the street. We finally have my mama back.

Friday
Today I was fired from my babysitting job. I packed up my things and hugged my little patient goodbye. What an experience we had. What an honor and a privilege it was to care for her. I will treasure these past 2 weeks forever. They say you can't go back home again. Sometimes they are wrong.

Now I am at the cabin and snuggled in my little loft bed with my laptop typing up the last journal entry of 'Life with Mother'. But something is off … this mattress is way too soft. We might have to make a trip to the gravel yard tomorrow.

Give me a sense of humor, Lord,
Give me the grace to see a joke,
To get some happiness from life,
And pass it on to other folk.

-Sir Thomas More